MW00777413

EXECUTIVE OFFICE

A Look at the U.S. Presidents
Through the Lens of Leadership

Tim Traudt

First Edition

ISBN: 978-1-66786-045-9 (paperback)

ISBN: 978-1-66786-046-6

Editing, layout, and typesetting by Yellow Barn Creative

DEDICATION

For Terri, whose passion for learning fuels my own
and whose love lights my way.

CONTENTS

FOREWORD

By Greg Carr

Throughout history, people have always faced significant challenges, confronted desperate circumstances, and needed strong leadership. Our present moment is one of those times as well. In my lifetime, nothing comes close to the visceral chasm that exists across our country today politically, socially, and spiritually. Great leadership can bridge those divides. That need for strong leadership extends beyond public office, as well, right into the boardrooms of many of our country's companies. Our country, workplaces, and communities desperately need and deserve strong leadership.

I'm a retired U.S. Navy officer, and I've had the privilege to work for and with extraordinary leaders during both my military service and my thirty-three years of corporate life. Tim Traudt, the author of this book, is right at the top of that list. I met Tim in 2008 and was fortunate enough to ultimately work directly for him. I got a front-row seat to see his true character, leadership skills, and outstanding style during times of stress and challenge. He is a man of unquestionable integrity. He consistently demonstrates moral courage and a deep understanding of accountability and responsibility. Every decision I observed Tim make was grounded in his solid leadership principles and foundational values.

In Executive Office, Tim has done something remarkable. By choosing to collect and share his ten leadership principles in this book, he has given current and future leaders a true gift: a path towards leading better.

But the book goes far beyond that. Tim's evaluation of the U.S. Presidents through the lens of his leadership principles is a fascinating read. What you have before you is part treatise on leadership development, part history lesson, and at all times an opportunity to reflect on what outstanding leadership should be. With hope it will be an inspiration for all those who share Tim's belief that "leadership is not a position but rather a responsibility" for a long time to come. I know it was for me.

Greg Carr is an Executive Vice President, Executive Director, Wealth Management at one of the top twenty-five banks in the United States and serves on the corporation's executive committee. Carr leads the Wealth and Investment Management business, serving the needs of high-net-worth clients and institutions.

Earlier in his career, he worked in wholesale banking, risk management, and market leadership roles. He retired from the United States Navy Reserve as a Lieutenant Commander with more than twenty-two years of dedicated service. He was awarded the Bronze Star Medal for his leadership in Operation Iraqi Freedom.

INTRODUCTION

"Curiosity is the wick in the candle of learning."
- William Arthur Ward

From an early age, when I self-declared myself mayor of the neighborhood dirt pile, to my final days in corporate America, leadership has been my passion. My love of history has developed more recently by reading hundreds of books—both non-fiction and historical fiction—while in the air logging countless airline miles and from my favorite reading spot on my porch in Minneapolis, Minnesota.

The Merriam-Webster dictionary defines a historian as "a student or writer of history; especially one who produces a scholarly synthesis." I am not a historian, nor do I pretend to be one, though I am a history lover and fascinated by historical trends. The dictionary defines a leader as "something or someone who leads." I am a leader. Much of my forty-year career working in the financial services industry, most recently as an Executive Vice President, allowed me the privilege of leading teams of various forms and sizes, from small to very large. In all, I had the privilege of leading thousands of people.

Several years ago, I decided to combine my love of history, specifically American history, with my passion for leadership. I wanted to take a closer look at our presidents, not just to better understand who these people were but also to evaluate them through the lens of leadership. So, I began a journey to get to know and better understand those who have held the highest executive office of the land: the office of president of the United States.

That journey spawned this book. In examining our nation's presidents, I continually found certain leadership tactics and techniques being employed to great success or overlooked to underwhelming results. I also started noticing that those techniques dovetailed with the same leadership principles I taught to others during my corporate career, principles that I think current leaders, whatever their field, can use to learn and grow.

In the following pages you'll meet forty-two of the forty-five people who have held the office of the presidency, from George Washington to George W. Bush. (Grover Cleveland held office twice on separated terms). Given that presidential papers—a collection of the writings, addresses, and remarks of a sitting president—are not released until twelve years after a president leaves office, Presidents Barack Obama, Donald Trump, and Joseph Biden have not had authorized biographies written about them yet. As a result, I have not included them here. In studying the U.S. presidents, I read a biography on each. Some of the biographies I chose were based on my level of interest in the president or the author. Each were long, deep stories of the person, covering where and how they grew up, who influenced them, and providing an overview of the political and economic situations of the day. Others were part of Macmillan's "The American Presidents" series. These were shorter books but gave a quality overview of who the men were, how they were shaped, and what they accomplished in office.

In addition to reviewing each president's key accomplishments and a few failures, I considered each through my own personal lens of leadership, broken out in ten principles. These are not exhaustive of all leadership characteristics, but they are ones that have guided me well through my career in corporate America.

In part one of the book, I have outlined these ten principles and presented how they are reflected in various presidents. In part two, I have ranked who I see as the top presidents based on their leadership abilities.

In part three, I've examined the bottom twelve. Finally, in part four, I've covered "the big middle," where most of us live as leaders. My hope is that the lessons and cautionary tales you take away from the top, middle, and bottom tiers of the presidents will allow you to improve your leadership skills as well.

Exploring the Office

No leader goes it alone.

The Constitution of the United States was established with a philosophical framework built on 1) cooperation, 2) compromise, and 3) consensus. Written in 1787, this founding document established the role of president as limited. In fact, it had the least impact of the three branches of government, after Legislative and Judicial. Decision-making in the new nation was designed to be a shared process.

At the same time, I've learned in my career just how important it is for leadership to have an accountable face. Article Two of the United States Constitution established the president as being 1) Commander in Chief, 2) Chief Executive Officer, 3) Chief Diplomat, 4) Chief Legislator, and 5) Chief of Staff.[1] Many of these roles were drafted based on what George Washington did and how he managed the office, including the forming of a cabinet.

Much like society, the office has evolved. There have been times in our nation's history when the public voted for, demanded, or needed a stronger executive. There were also times when the president pushed his power beyond the scope of the Constitution and gains in authority were temporary. There were other times when a current occupant permanently pushed the authority of the office for future presidents.

Of the 42 U.S. presidents covered in this book, fourteen served two full terms in office, seven served one term plus varied additional months or years up to their death or resignation, twelve served one term, and nine

---

1 U.S. Const. art. II.

served less than one term (again, up to their death or resignation). President Franklin D. Roosevelt served 4,422 days, the longest, and William Henry Harrison served thirty-one days, the shortest. Eight of our presidents died while in office; four were assassinated and four died of illness.

For most of the presidents, leadership was a skill honed prior to holding the office. Many presidents were previous governors, senators, or served in the U.S. House of Representatives. Several held cabinet or ministry/ambassador roles before holding the executive office. Some were military leaders. Some were businessmen. Nearly half were lawyers. John Quincy Adams served in the House of Representatives after he was president, and John Tyler served in the Confederate States Congress after serving the Union as president. William Taft was the only president to later become a Supreme Court justice. Generally, all presidents saw their role as being a servant of the people. How they chose to play that role out was based on their style, the country's circumstances, whether their party was in control, and how they viewed the likelihood of reelection.

Exploring the Rankings

Rating the presidents, like eating "good" food or drink, clearly involves biases. My rankings are measured against the criteria established by historical scholars. Historical perspective is also considered, as it is impossible to judge each president based on the generally accepted norms of today considering the evolution of social and political views over the past 240-plus years. Think of how our country's views on slavery, women's rights, labor laws, and technology have changed! As public opinion played a significant role in impacting each of the president's policies and platforms, I assessed each leader using the prevailing public opinion of the day, whether it was acceptable or not using our current social lens. I've done my best to be non-partisan. Not only have the parties changed significantly over time, but leadership is not bound by political parties.

When reviewing historians' consensus of "greatest presidents," I found common personality characteristics. The top-tier presidents left us with lessons for being successful. Their characteristics included humility, charisma, administrative skill, clear communication, a sense of calm in difficult times, and respect for the office. They had the ability to serve all people and played the "long game" for the country.

Historians judged the "worst presidents" not only by what they did but what they failed to do. This bottom tier shared personality characteristics as well. Most were self-serving, arrogant, stubborn, and spineless when it came to tough decisions. They tended to be narrow or limited in their thinking when they desperately needed perspective. Most who failed surrounded themselves with corrupt or inept talent (friends or those they owed favors) or tried to do too much alone.

In my ranking of the best and worst presidents, I used criteria and categories that have been used since the first presidential ranking was conducted in 1948 by Arthur M. Schlesinger of Harvard University. These evolving polls have typically been completed every twelve years or so. Most polls have changed to become less politically biased. Polls that revealed political favoritism were discarded. Historians' opinions have varied over the years, as has the number of polling members. Today the number of most respected historians is smaller and only comprises highly published prominent authorities.[2]

At a macro level, the three primary themes for historical judgment of a president are 1) Is the nation stronger and more respected today than before, 2) Is the office of the president stronger than when they entered the office, and 3) Did they rise to extraordinary heights during extraordinary challenges?

It's tempting to try to measure everyone and everything off clear and measurable data points. When evaluating leadership skills, it is important

---

2 "2021 Presidential Historians Survey." C-SPAN. https://www.c-span.org/presidentsurvey2021/?page=overall.

to look at the lasting impact. Actions both great and small can have long-term or even permanent effects on society or business. I have attempted to bring out these issues as best I can for each president.

I have evaluated the presidents not as a scholar or judge but as a citizen, a leader, and someone who loves history. While I have attempted to be fair and unbiased in my own rankings, I haven't entirely succeeded. When evaluated through the lens of leadership, some presidents captured my imagination and respect far more than others. My hope is you will enjoy this book and find value in my observations, assessments, and insights. After all, if you've found your way to these pages, there's a good chance you're in a leadership role yourself.

PART ONE

The Ten Principles of Leadership

CHAPTER 1

Leadership Lasts for Life

MANY YEARS AGO, WHEN I was leading a group of sales and service professionals, I was asked to speak at a developing leader's program we offered at the large midwestern regional bank where I worked. I had never consciously articulated the fundamental principles of my leadership style. But these principles were clear in my mind, so I jotted them down beforehand. They impacted my audience more than I or the program director anticipated. She extended the session well beyond the scheduled time and I was asked to share them again and again at leadership meetings and presentations over the next 30-plus years. Several times I refreshed them to incorporate the latest buzz words of the day, only to go back to the original "dead sea scrolls," as my longtime colleagues would joke, that I first introduced to a group of aspiring influencers.

Knowing the impact any of us can have on others is so important. As people, and as leaders, we're influenced by behaviors we observe, both good and bad. Our encouragement or discouragement during times in our lives impacts our future choices. Think about individuals, events, and social movements that profoundly impacted your life. Now think about the leaders who were at the heart of those moments.

The long-term impact of a leader is something we tend to lose sight of in the moment and later reflect on over time. I've heard countless stories about people who left a profession, quit an instrument or sport, or still had an inferiority complex because of the influence of a few. Likewise, I've heard how a mentor, friend, or manager's encouragement dramatically changed a person's life for the good. I personally chose my profession because an adjunct professor encouraged me to get into banking. He told me I would be an outstanding banker and as a twenty-year-old economics and business major I believed him. On the flip side, I cowered in applying for advanced opportunities early in my career when mediocre managers told me I wasn't qualified. We all have leadership opportunities and can make a difference in those we encounter. The question is how we will use these opportunities.

Leadership evolves, as does thinking. Never changing course or shifting one's opinion is detrimental to yourself and those you lead. Core principles and beliefs may evolve, but they rarely seem to drift much beyond their foundation. They define us as individuals and leaders.

In reading and reflecting on historians' rankings of the best and worst U.S. Presidents, I found I wanted to go beyond the critics' recognizable criteria. I wanted to look at them through the lens of leadership that shaped my career. While I fully appreciate that since the beginning of time, both men and women have successfully led people using different core characteristics and principles, my principles—developed in the late twentieth century in a capitalist democracy—were quite effective and rarely disputed, at least to my face. It was through this lens I evaluated the presidents.

It was more than thirty years ago when I first captured these guiding principles I followed as a leader. I realized all of them would require me to continue to learn and grow. I never felt I would master any of them and I never have. What they did was guide and challenge me to continually grow and mature in each area. Even now, in my post-corporate life, my goal is to continue to hone these skills. Learning is a lifetime sport!

CHAPTER 2

Principle One –

Care for the Flock, Not the Fleece

THIS FIRST PRINCIPLE ESSENTIALLY asks, "who do I serve, and why do I serve?" All the presidents I ranked in my top twelve had a profound sense of the enormity of who they were serving. Many historians believe that as few as one-half of U.S. presidents enjoyed the responsibilities of the office. The other half perceived the immense responsibility as a challenge they would not wish on anyone. Furthermore, the responsibilities and demands on the president of the United States far exceed what they are compensated for the job.

The role does create unique challenges, given the balance of power and the need to keep your party in a power position. I believe recent presidents especially have become more of a slave to their party than a steward to the entire population they are called to serve. George Washington warned of this in his farewell address in 1796.

Staying in power can become more important than doing the right thing for many wayward leaders, no matter their industry. As a leader, I believe it is critically important to know who you are truly serving and always consider that population before making significant decisions. I also believe there should be standards that you won't breach. For example, most companies say their people are their "secret sauce"—until they run into tough times. Then, suddenly, wages, benefits, training, and headcounts start to be seen as expendable expenses.

Saying you believe in or support something and doing something to demonstrate it are often two different things. Knowing who you serve and why you serve informs both the head and heart of a leader. Authentic leadership requires this alignment of "head and heart." One must ask oneself, "what is the intention of my service?" If the answer is to serve your ego, that's all you will satisfy. If it is to serve others, you have built the foundation of authentic leadership.

Harry Truman was a presidential example of someone who excelled at "caring for the flock" leadership. He famously introduced himself to and knew the names of every staff member in his administration. Throughout his presidency, he would call members of his cabinet to his office, reminding them that they were there to serve the needs of everyday people.

At the heart of what motivates a leader and why they serve will ultimately dictate their behaviors. Servant leaders are motivated by meeting the needs of others.

Several years ago, the president of our division decided to create a formal leadership development program. He chose me and a couple of my colleagues to build and implement the program. This program lasted for several years. Despite continual challenges to "improve efficiencies" (a fancy term for cutting expenses), our president considered it foundational and continued to invest in it. "Caring for the flock" is not just a cute slogan; it means genuinely investing in people, careers, and lives.

CHAPTER 3

Principle Two –

Create and Communicate

a Vision and Plan

I FREQUENTLY SHARE AN old saying with leaders: "If you're leading and no one is following, you're only taking a walk." Great leaders have a vision for their team, their organization, and even their country. Strategies and tactics should be guided by and designed to align with this vision. Ideally, this vision is consistent, concise, and repeatable. It should be at the heart of the organization's mission and something that is truly believable and achievable.

Visions and plans can evolve, though. Abraham Lincoln's vision is a great example. His vision was to ultimately hold our Union together. He evolved and expanded on this vision to make good on the truth set forth in the U.S. Declaration of Independence that all men were created equal by issuing the Emancipation Proclamation. While this emancipation of slaves in the rebelling states was an executive order (using war powers), it forced the issue of ultimately freeing all people from the ugly bondage that gripped and divided our nation from its very beginning.

Lincoln's vision was the light that led this country through its darkest hour. Consider the several presidents who served just before him and many that followed. They faced the same core issue of slavery, but they did so with no vision, no courage, and limited followership, which is both the capacity and willingness to follow a leader. Their records reflect their lack of vision and subsequent failure.

Eisenhower was known to be a meticulous planner and executor of strategies and tactics. His military experience greatly benefited his ability to analyze priorities and create accountabilities to complete the task.

Of all the presidents, though, it was George Washington who truly had a vision and saw the landscape the clearest. Washington's wisdom to understand how he acted and operated in office would be a template for future presidents is indeed an example of a long-view leader. His acts of stepping down, first as the head of the army and then the presidency so the country could move forward, were unheard of, selfless, and truly an act many leaders could learn from today.

Early in my career, I played golf with a college friend who owned a consulting company. He shared with me the challenge he had when working with companies that not only didn't connect vision to strategies or tactics but didn't seem even to know the difference. I listened intently, secretly thinking, "I'm not sure our business understands the difference, let alone makes it a practice!" In the future, connecting every strategy to the corporate business vision became the habit I instilled. Furthermore, we ensured each tactic aligned with a strategy. Doing this gave each team member a better sense of how their work helped achieve the organization's vision.

It surprises me how seldom leaders tie strategies and tactics to the overall vision. Here's what we are doing, here's why we are doing it, here's how we will do it, and here's when. Too often, we see actions as a series of independent behaviors, never really connecting what one is called to do and how it impacts the overall mission. Imagine the ownership you can get when people believe and see their contribution matters!

CHAPTER 4

Principle Three – Focus on a Few Well-Done Items to Make a Big Difference

IT'S EASY FOR LEADERS to have too many priorities and goals. As much as we think we can multitask and be good at everything, typically we can't and aren't. By taking on overly large agendas, we end up stretching people's energy and our own reserves to the point where nothing is done well.

It's also important to be able to measure the results of a priority. If it's important, measure your progress. One of the best rules of thumb is "if we accomplish this task, assignment, or goal, it will significantly improve our business." Each worthwhile discipline or practice should truly make the larger organization better.

Most priorities require the alignment and cooperation of others. Many times these individuals or groups are not under your authority or influence. I always encourage leaders to "play chess, not checkers." That means they don't have to always "win" an immediate issue but instead should keep their eyes on the longer-range strategic plan. Most of the time that requires them to build allies. Great leaders must choose not to "die on every hill" but instead know when to let partners or even adversaries feel heard, become trusted, and even "win a few." The great presidents, like all great leaders, understood this and rose above partisanship.

It is not to say that every bill or appointment isn't important, but there are typically only a few significant opportunities and impacts that a leader can make. We certainly see this with the marginal changes most presidents were able to accomplish during their administration. Most leaders try to distinguish themselves by changing or overriding what their predecessor put in place. Sometimes that is warranted. Often, it's only ego, an inflated sense of self, directed at other people. On the other hand, confidence is a natural expression of ability, expertise, and self-regard. Don't confuse the two!

Lyndon Johnson was a master at this. He started as a leader in the Senate, constantly pushing to accomplish what the president's agenda was, even if it meant it wasn't exactly like he would have done it. When he became president himself, the allies he built and his consistency of "playing chess" allowed him to pass the Civil Rights Act of 1964, a long-overdue law.

One of the things I learned from reading the presidential biographies is how few long-lasting impacts each president can accomplish. There are checks and balances, partisanship, unanticipated events, and the fact that campaign promises don't always make sense when you learn the realities of the office.

The CEO of our company once walked into my office and saw my to-do list proudly displayed on two flip charts. He asked me, "Which one of these items would make the biggest difference to your business if you did it really well?" I pointed out two. He said, "Why are you wasting your time trying to do the others? I pay you too much to work on things you should delegate." I didn't think it was an appropriate time to debate my pay, but he certainly made a lasting point. I learned to filter and put my energy where it mattered most.

CHAPTER 5

Principle Four –

Always Know Your Audience

REMEMBER THAT LEADERSHIP IS a speaking role, and communication is like any other muscle we have. It needs to be continually developed and strengthened. To be effective, one doesn't need to be an extrovert, have a great stage presence, or an abundance of charisma. Great communicators understand their audience and the landscape of any given room they're in. They have a point. They set and reinforce expectations by first telling us what they are going to tell us, then telling us, and then finishing by telling us what they told us.

Honing your communication skills is essential to creating followership. I'm amazed how many leaders are ill-prepared to say even a few words to the people they're in charge of managing. "Winging it" often makes you look like a fool. And not relating to your audience makes you look tone-deaf.

Most of our presidents were good or excellent communicators. While today campaigning is critical to getting elected, that wasn't always the case. The art of communication and relating to an audience are two characteristics that both Theodore (Teddy) and Franklin D. Roosevelt (FDR) were known for. Teddy's optimism and vitality made him a popular leader. He was seen as strong and courageous, which was greatly admired in society at the turn of the century. FDR's famous fireside chats gave millions of Americans hope during the Great Depression and World War II.

People trusted him. He spoke directly to them, and, as a result, he greatly expanded the power of the office, pushing through the New Deal—the most extensive social safety net in U.S. history. Despite being a country made up of independent people, by trusting FDR, the country voluntarily and significantly shifted toward "big government." Before that, expanded government would not have been embraced.

John F. Kennedy (JFK) famously used his communication skills to press the country into service with the Peace Corp. His charismatic style ushered in an era of "Camelot," a mythical realm of King Arthur reflecting an aura of youth, vigor, and shiny virtue.

Ronald Reagan was another excellent communicator. His command and presence brought optimism and hope in a time when Americans felt their status on the world stage was fading.

Public speaking is a very difficult exercise for most of us. I always felt you needed to be an extrovert to be a good public speaker. I also thought that all leaders were outstanding communicators. I mean they had to be to be in that role, right? I was wrong—they're not! One of the best pieces of advice I ever received was to continually grow as a communicator. From a beginning acting class in college to personal coaching after a presentation, I have been repeatedly reminded to be prepared, practice, be clear and concise, know your audience and, if possible, inspire. While not an all-inclusive list of elements of excellent public speaking, these few tips can go a long way.

CHAPTER 6

Principle Five – Avoid Hubris

AS A LEADER, I implore you to take your task seriously, but yourself not too seriously.

Competence is one of the core attributes of a great leader. But too often, *confidence* is misinterpreted as *competence*. Many leaders have failed because they perceive an inflated sense of self-greatness. Take the leader who lets the praise go to their heads and starts believing all their ideas are truly brilliant. It's a slippery slope to hubris and disaster.

The more prudent play is to take yourself and your accomplishments with a grain of salt. Be humble, above all else. And be open to the idea that you might not be the smartest person in every room. The reality is that most leaders surround themselves with like-minded people and hate to get bad news. When this occurs, they can become reckless with pride. In Greek Mythology, Icarus pridefully flew too close to the sun with his wax wings. Like Icarus, these leaders often tumble from the sky and drown as well.

Many presidents have fallen prey to this type of thinking due to the nature of the office and who they surrounded themselves with. Some, like Thomas Jefferson, Woodrow Wilson, and Lyndon Johnson, let their egos impact their effectiveness and legacy.

I believe humor makes us more human and thus more relatable. People follow those they believe in. Those leaders who understand their weaknesses, accept criticism, manage praise, can defuse tension with humor, and constantly learn from experience and others, stand to make the most positive impact.

James Monroe, Teddy Roosevelt, Calvin Coolidge, Harry Truman, Dwight Eisenhower, Gerald Ford, and Ronald Reagan understood humility. They used humor frequently, often self-deprecating, to lighten moments and work through tense issues.

I'll never forget the first leader I worked for who could laugh at himself, readily admitted to and learned from his mistakes, and humbly gave credit to others when things went well. I learned the most from him of any leader I ever worked for. His approach and style gave his team confidence and the freedom to occasionally fail. We did fail at times but learned from the experience and continued to get better. Humbleness doesn't mean weakness; it means confidence despite imperfection.

CHAPTER 7

Principle Six – Maintain Balance and Don't Waste a Good Worry

REGARDLESS OF THE CONSEQUENCES, many leaders seem to throw everything into their work and leave little or no time for other important aspects of their lives. Being a great leader requires that you can finish the race. Leadership, especially in times of crisis, can be incredibly stressful. Managing multiple tasks as well as diverse interests and needs can be overwhelming. We all know stories of careers being cut short because of burnout.

Worry won't change outcomes. Being concerned, being prepared, and being cautious are very important. Great leaders understand and respect risk. Worry can become an obsession and consume you, yet not being concerned enough can destroy you. It's important to understand that fine line and try not to see everything as "life or death"—it's not.

Work-life balance is a worthy goal. It has also been an overplayed buzz phrase in the workplace since the late twentieth century. Balance in life is something companies tend to talk—a lot—about but it's never really rewarded. Working weekends, missing vacations, taking calls and messages at all hours of the day and night can be seen as a badge of honor. Balance doesn't mean equal. Work and sleep alone can eat up almost the full twenty-four hours of any day. What I've discovered about balance is the importance of being "present" in the mode of activity you're in at any given time. If it is family, put down the phone and be there. Fitness? Don't run on your treadmill during a conference call. Spiritual? Be silent, pray, read, and join in fellowship with a singular focus.

U.S. Presidents are by design always "on call," and some made little time for life outside of the office. Yet many looked to maintain a manageable work-life balance. Teddy Roosevelt was an avid sportsman who prided himself in an active life, as did John F. Kennedy (to the level his disabilities allowed). Ronald Reagan was famous for his controlled workday and afternoon nap. Abraham Lincoln, Franklin Roosevelt, Harry Truman, and Lyndon Johnson lived for their job. Their health and family life paid dearly.

The leader sets the tone on balance. In the '80-'90s working Saturdays and late was a badge of honor in our organization. I'm sure we weren't unique. I missed a lot of quality time, either physically or mentally not being present. It is one of the biggest regrets of my career. It is what I thought I needed to do to show I was committed and hungry. It wasn't until I was applying for a regional position, after a company merger, that the new group head who was interviewing me asked two questions in my interview. Where did I grow up? And did I work my way through college? Seriously, I had literally memorized the financial results of my business, and strategies I was going to implement if I got the job and he wanted to know about my janitorial job in college. He said I can read about your results, and I can find out if you're a good partner with one phone call. How you speak about your family and your ability to work tells me you're organized and will work hard. He spent the entire time talking about his family and a health scare he had. While I'm not sure these are the best screening questions to judge an executive's success, they did remind me that being successful was about a lot more than working Saturdays. I began to change my work habits to be more balanced, to be more present, and create priorities outside of work because the leader's attitude made it okay. He gave me a gift.

We like to think we can "have it all." We can't. We can manage multiple priorities, but great leaders focus on balance. They appropriately delegate tasks and priorities. They expand themselves by learning, forming trusting and loving relationships, exercising their bodies, eating well, and drinking moderately, and getting their sleep. Science is now confirming something I've always cherished: sleep is essential!

As my responsibilities expanded throughout my career, I needed to become more deliberate about managing my work-life balance. I realized that imbalance and worry were directly correlated. I observed individuals who seemed more relaxed and at peace than I was and emulated them. One of the practices I employed was cutting off calls and meetings early Friday afternoons. That included staying off emails—or at least attempting to. While not revolutionary, that allowed me to decompress as I headed into the weekend and restore more quickly. While worry was always lurking, it became much more manageable when I was rested. I also had two excellent people who helped and supported me continually around balance: my wife and an outstanding executive assistant. I highly recommend caring accountability partners!

You've only got one life. Make the most of it. Respect yourself and enjoy living. The work will always be there and will continue long after you're gone.

CHAPTER 8

Principle Seven –

Be Curious and Continue to Learn

ARISTOTLE IS CREDITED WITH saying, "The more you know, the more you realize you don't know." Continually learning, experiencing, and opening yourself up to different views make you more interesting and ultimately more interested. One of the reasons people don't learn is they surround themselves with like-minded people and don't respect the opinions of others. This is symptomatic of a lack of trust, insecurity, or being afraid of being disagreed with or challenged. And I've always believed if you can't trust, you can't be trusted.

One of the most powerful statements a leader can tell a subordinate is, "I trust your decision." Creating an environment of trust, allowing for mistakes, and learning from them will enable personal growth and develop those around you. It will also help you keep a flexible mindset and avoid rigid thinking.

Great Leaders are constantly learning and evolving. Abraham Lincoln was a classic example of this, as his thoughts on slavery evolved significantly throughout his time in office.

Another key to being a great leader is learning to be a great coach. Many confuse coaching with management and don't appreciate the art of coaching. I've had the privilege of working with and learning from some outstanding coaches. The best coaches are great listeners, they ask questions and listen to the answer (quite a novel idea!). Managing a conversation is not listening but more likely telling. Knowing when to invoke either skill is vital for leaders. It is crucial to understand whether the decision-making process should approach a situation as a coach, manager, or leader. One size doesn't fit all! Unfortunately, many organizations either don't value coaching, place it as an ambiguous category for their leaders, or believe that at executive levels it's unnecessary. I would argue that great leaders invest in it, encourage its development, and lead from the front as examples. People leave managers; they rarely leave leaders.

One of the development tools we adopted at our company was Gallup StrengthsFinder. This is an excellent resource that identifies an individual's top five personal strengths. One of my top strengths was identified as "learner." That didn't surprise me, as I was always reading and observing practices and concepts from a broad spectrum of industries, looking for ways to improve our business. Fortunately, several like-minded colleagues were also exploring service models. Curiosity and observation led us to a unique delivery model for how we holistically served our clients. Ironically, our best learnings didn't come from our own industry but from the health care industry. Never be afraid to leverage the brilliant work of others.

CHAPTER 9

Principle Eight – Build Followership

AN AFRICAN PROVERB SAYS, "If you understand in your head and believe in your heart, you will follow with your feet." Too often, leaders confuse understanding with believing. We think somehow because we simply say something, it will automatically be followed.

According to the Meriam-Webster Dictionary, followership is "the capacity or willingness to follow a leader." It doesn't occur naturally based on authority or hierarchy. True followership is earned and requires confidence and trust in the leader. Leaders with strong character and high integrity are much more likely to be followed than those who lack decency.

Consider the challenges when introducing a new strategy. How do you get people to follow? To achieve sustainable followership, one must connect the strategy to the classic questions of "what, why, when, where, and how." This simple road map also allows the leader to connect the dots around vision, strategy, and tactics. If you want people to be more than mercenaries, this is essential. You need to connect the head, heart, and "feet."

While incentives are valuable, it's important not to rely on financial incentives alone to drive behavior. Competitors can easily match an incentive. Most people stay with an organization and follow their leaders because they understand and believe in the mission and their role in executing it. Followership requires belief. Unless forced, people rarely follow those we don't have faith in.

Building followership is critical at both the individual and group levels. One of the most important gifts a leader can bring to their organization is the effective development of their team. Great leaders surround themselves with outstanding talent. They continually develop others and give them opportunities to grow and shine.

Leaders own the culture of the organization. Without a strong culture, no strategy will exist for long. Building a culture is a long-term, critical effort that needs continual alignment, understanding, and trust. Many organizations understand this and successfully embrace it. Unfortunately, others simply go through the motions.

Theodore Roosevelt was known to make projects happen and Franklin Roosevelt greatly expanded the role of government. In each instance, the country followed with their vote. Followership matters!

I learned the "followership matters" lesson the hard way. I mistook agreement and lack of resistance as a sign of followership. It wasn't until I got results from a 360-degree review (a process where your direct reports and peers review your performance) that I realized several key people were not only not following my lead, but they didn't even fully understand the initiative we were trying to complete. I had mistakenly thought that everyone would naturally be on board because I understood it, and I was the boss. I had never fully communicated the value and importance of the initiative, thereby giving them a chance to understand and believe its significance. That was a big miss I tried not to repeat! If you want to have followership, you've got be a leader worth following.

CHAPTER 10

Principle Nine – Be Courageous

LEADERSHIP IS NOT A position; it's a responsibility. We see it shine or fade during difficult times. Leadership requires courage. Courage to place the right people in the right role at the right time. Courage to defend. Courage to rebuild when necessary. Too many times, we look to fix the symptom and not the cause. Great Leaders get to root problems and make tough, often unpopular decisions.

It's easy to default to what's popular versus necessary when setting an agenda or making changes. But the ultimate judge is outcomes, not what was the popular opinion of the time. Throughout history, we've seen Presidents excel when they demonstrated courage and fail when they didn't. For example, many early presidents put their heads in the sand around the issue of slavery, which eventually led to civil war.

Courage manifests itself in both what we do and don't do. John Adams avoided a war and lost a chance at a second term. Andrew Jackson created the Second National Bank, which consolidated power away from private banks. Thomas Jefferson and James Polk greatly expanded the size of our country while we were a relatively new experiment. Ulysses S. Grant reinforced reconstruction and promoted civil rights. These are several examples that had both popular and unpopular sentiments.

Knowing and believing in what you are trying to accomplish also requires trust in yourself. I love to play golf. If I'm not playing well or the weather conditions are challenging—not uncommon in Minneapolis—I often forgo my fundamentals and stop trusting my swing. It's no different in leadership; we tend not to keep our head and trust the foundational vision and mission when times are tough. Avoid that temptation. Be courageous.

CHAPTER 11

Principle Ten – Brand Matters

WHEN YOU'RE A LEADER, the microphone—or should I say iPhone—is always on. People with influence are watched, listened to, and copied. It's imperative to craft, cultivate, own, and protect your personal brand.

Jeff Bezos, the founder of Amazon, describes a personal brand as "what people say about you when you are not in the room." We all know how important a brand is. Unfortunately, it takes years to create and only one or two missteps to destroy. Yet failures in life are inevitable, and we will all experience them at some point. Our ability to admit our mistakes, accept blame and set a new course will have as much long-term impact on our brand as being angry, defensive, or anything less than authentic.

What do you think of when you think of George Washington? Father of our country, chopped down a cherry tree, never told a lie? Abraham Lincoln—honest? Harry Truman—the buck stops here? John F. Kennedy—Camelot? Richard Nixon—Watergate? That's brand!

Leaders' brands are inextricable from their company's brands, and vice versa. I spent most of my career at a large financial services company with an iconic brand. We even had a TV show about us in the late 1950s and 60s. Then, in a season of misaligned incentives and poor oversight, the actions of a few caused significant damage to our brand. Individuals within the company paid a steep price. Repairing a damaged brand is a highly arduous, painful, and lengthy process, but worth the effort.

One of the questions to ask oneself is what do you truly want to be known for and why? Personal brand is so precious and precarious. Building it, knowing it, and protecting it is essential.

PART TWO

The Top U.S. Presidents Through

the Lens of Leadership

CHAPTER 12

Thoughts on the Top

MY TOP GROUP OF twelve U.S. Presidents shares several leadership characteristics. First and foremost, they saw their role as "stewardship." They generally served a broader audience beyond their party (at least in appearance) to make the lives of all Americans safe and prosperous. They had a vision. They had a grasp of the big picture and still sought out and considered smaller details. They led from the front. They were widely respected internationally and have generally stood the test of time.

Most historians judge the presidents on core qualities such as communication and managerial skill. It isn't easy to compare these skills over hundreds of years. The evolving complexities of the office and the advancement of communication tools available to them make such comparisons nearly impossible. I have assessed communication by the methods of the day and managerial skills on outcomes rather than approach. After the first five "founding" presidents, it's apparent that most were judged by popular vote on their communication and likeability. Some, such as Polk, Lincoln, Teddy Roosevelt, Franklin Roosevelt, and Kennedy, did an excellent job connecting with the public. Washington was known for being well-spoken in his day, too. As for managerial skills, those who sought out the best talent for various jobs and positions as opposed to granting political favors were most effective.

These presidents all appeared to have good intentions and tried to do what was best for the country. Those with vision and courage proved to be the most successful. It is clear the overly cautious, as well as those who were more interested in staying in office, were less successful. It's also clear that a few squandered their places in history.

Judging the best of the group requires a longer view of history. Some of these top presidents served in times of economic expansion and relative international peace and prosperity, which is a great advantage to both the job and the ability to build a positive legacy. Some made outstanding cabinet picks or Supreme Court appointments that helped shape our country. On the flip side, some inherited a mess, faced war or difficult economies, and worked their way out of more significant problems, and thus are recognized for those accomplishments. Bills and policies that didn't have a profound or lasting impact on the country, such as tax changes or regulatory amendments, were not given much credit.

In the book of Esther in the Old Testament of the Bible, Mordecai, an advisor to Queen Esther, spoke of a dire situation and ended with the question, "And who knows but that you have come to your royal position for such a time as this?" The top presidents, who served in the most difficult times, boldly led in "such a time as this."

Top Twelve Presidents Ranked Through the Lens of Leadership

1.	Abraham Lincoln	1861-1865, Republican, elected for two terms, assassinated while in office, 16th president
2.	George Washington	1789-1797, no party affiliation, elected for two terms, 1st president
3.	Theodore Roosevelt	1901-1909, Republican, served remaining term of William McKinley, elected for one term, 26th president
4.	Franklin D. Roosevelt	1933-1945, Democrat, elected for four terms, died in office, 32nd president
5.	Thomas Jefferson	1801-1809, Democratic-Republican, elected for two terms, 3rd president
6.	Harry Truman	1945-1953, Democrat, served remaining term of Franklin Roosevelt, elected for one term, 33rd president
7.	Dwight Eisenhower	1953-1961, Republican, elected for two terms, 34th president
8.	Lyndon B. Johnson	1965-1969, Democrat, served remaining term of Kennedy, elected for one term, 36th president
9.	Woodrow Wilson	1913-1921, Democrat, elected for two terms, 28th president
10.	James Monroe	1817-1825, Democratic-Republican, elected for two terms, 5th president
11.	James Polk	1845-1849, Democrat, elected for one term, 11th president
12.	John F. Kennedy	1961-1963, Democrat, elected for one term, assassinated while in office, 35th president

CHAPTER 13

HONEST ABE

Abraham Lincoln, 1861-1865

OUR 16TH PRESIDENT WAS one of the least prepared for the office. Born and raised in poverty, Abraham Lincoln was a self-taught lawyer by trade who continually indulged in learning. He deeply studied law, military strategy, and the Constitution. He was incredibly smart and an outstanding communicator. He was elected to the U.S. House of Representatives from Illinois in 1846 and to the presidency in 1860. Lincoln placed his opponents in his cabinet — something only a few presidents have ever done.

Throughout his time in office, Lincoln's thinking evolved, and his priorities shifted from the goal of saving the union to the abolition of slavery. There is much debate about how much he detested slavery and what emancipation accomplished. Still, Lincoln took on what the founders failed to do. He cleverly abolished slavery in border states that had seceded from the union via executive order. This weakened the impacted states and challenged the contention that staying in the war wasn't about slavery. That view was a losing proposition after four years of civil war.

Confederate General Robert E. Lee officially surrendered the Army of Northern Virginia to Union General Ulysses S. Grant on April 9, 1865, effectively ending the civil war. Lincoln's orders to Grant were to "bind up the nation's wounds and unite the country." He didn't seek vengeance. It would only last briefly, as he was assassinated just five days later. I have no doubt that had Lincoln lived out the next four years, civil rights would have significantly advanced and the country, North and South, reconciled much earlier and with less animosity and strife. Instead, it took one hundred years for an actual civil rights bill to be passed.

While most of Lincoln's Presidency centered around the civil war, he also passed the first Homestead Act, allowing poor people to acquire land; established the U.S. Department of Agriculture; signed the Morrill Land Grant Act, which led to the creation of numerous universities; signed the Revenue Act of 1862, which ultimately led to the formation of the Internal Revenue Service; and established the U.S. National Banking System, which established a national currency and uniform banking policy. He was clearly a once-in-the-life-of-our-country leader.

Lessons in Leadership

Lincoln was a great communicator. He was clear, concise, and related to the audience. His most notable and quoted speech, the Gettysburg Address, lasted less than three minutes and had fewer than 275 words. Furthermore, he was incredibly courageous. The issue of slavery had plagued the country from its earliest days. Lincoln addressed this core problem and fought to preserve the Union. He chose the best people for cabinet roles, and they weren't always from his own party — some were his foes.

Lincoln was also not afraid to make tough decisions around leadership. He appointed General Grant head of the Union Army, even when critics disagreed. Surrounding yourself with the best people, regardless of whether their values or views match yours, is one of the most important things any leader can do. Great leaders choose the best in the field; not the "next in line."

True character reveals itself in the worst times, and throughout his presidency, Lincoln led with empathy. Great leaders foster followership by demonstrating empathy, which creates loyalty.

Great leaders also understand the value of having a clear vision and continually connect the strategies and tactics they implement to this vision. Clarity of vision is invaluable. Having a team that knows how their roles fit into the vision, strategy and tactics give organizations an incredible advantage. Lincoln showed a strong sense of vision and evolving strategy and tactics that led the country through our darkest hours.

For all his leadership gifts, Lincoln also showed us the downside of not maintaining any form of balance in life. He was wed to his job. The task in front of him was immense, yet so were the needs of his family, who were largely left unattended. Balance doesn't mean equal. The real lesson is finding the most treasured things and people in your life. Some things may need to be paused for a season. Lincoln ignored many important areas of his personal life. It's a common mistake, and one I've admittedly made myself on occasion.

CHAPTER 14

THE FATHER OF HIS COUNTRY

George Washington, 1789-1797

SO MANY THINGS ABOUT General George Washington's story are what legends are made of. He was a wealthy Virginian, Commander in Chief of the first Continental Army, and the first president of the newly formed United States of America. He had no blueprint for the presidency, yet he set a course of behavioral practices that are followed to this day.

The U.S. Constitution laid out the framework for governing the nation. Even today, the executive branch is the least defined of the three branches of government (Executive, Legislative, and Judicial). Much of the role of president was established based on standards set by George Washington. The fact that many of his protocols are followed still today speaks to the wisdom of having selected Washington as our first president.

A semi-aristocratic couple, George Washington and his wife Martha were at the forefront of events that shaped history. Together they made the office a respected symbol to the world as well as to the new country.

In addition to defining the office, the Bill of Rights was passed during Washington's presidency, as was the Judiciary Act of 1791, which established the federal judiciary of the United States, and the Bank Bill of 1791, which established the first Bank of the United States. During his two terms, he defined the expectations of the office while also keeping America out of the French Revolutionary Wars, which was no small task given France's support of the United States during our revolution. He also facilitated the

Treaty of San Lorenzo (also known as Pickney's Treaty, after Washington empowered envoy Thomas Pickney to negotiate terms), which peacefully settled a border dispute with Spain.

Lessons in Leadership

George Washington's first cabinet was a combination of rivals who held differing views on how the new country should operate. He demonstrated a commitment to bring in the best. Washington managed the differences among his cabinet members because of the high respect they had for him as a general. I find it interesting that the top two presidents were among the few who chose a cabinet representing diverse parties and interests other than their own personal views. This could serve as a lesson for current and future leaders!

Washington's attention to detail in developing the office was also impressive. Many leaders forget they are serving for a period and not forever. What they build for the future is as important as the results they generate during their time in power.

Like all great leaders, Washington chose to serve a cause bigger than himself. Rarely do people with such power and influence step down from that position for the good of the whole. Not only did Washington have incredible power—he was unanimously elected to office by the electoral college—but also immense wealth. The two combined could have easily caused him to not hassle with the challenges he faced throughout his presidency.

Without question, Washington built the most influential and powerful brand of all U.S. presidents. The biggest stain on his legacy is that he didn't free his slaves, even after his death. His brand was so powerful that had he done so, maybe others would have followed suit and the issue of slavery resolved long before a civil war.

CHAPTER 15

THE COLONEL

Theodore Roosevelt, 1901-1909

THEODORE ("TEDDY") ROOSEVELT BECAME the 26th president of the United States somewhat unexpectedly. Prior to his presidency, he had served as governor of New York and vice president of the United States. He became president following the assassination of President William McKinley in September 1901.

Teddy was an interesting character. When he became president at just forty-three years old, he was big, strong, athletic, and full of vigor. He was a populist conservative who strongly believed in and promoted state powers and limited federal government. He was a conservationist, and his legacy of creating and preserving national parks is a lasting gift to our country. He was also an advocate for women's rights who helped set the stage for women getting the right to vote during the Wilson administration less than a decade later.

Teddy not only supported labor but went further to force changes to child labor laws and unfair worker practices. Under his leadership, international transportation was forever changed with the construction of the Panama Canal, which strengthened trade and commerce between the Atlantic and Pacific Oceans. He improved consumer safety with the passage of the Food and Drug Act (FDA) and increased the regulatory power over railroads with the Interstate Commerce Commission.

Teddy's downside was Teddy. His ego often got in the way. After failing to receive the Replication nomination for reelection in 1912, he formed his own party, the Progressive Party, and nicknamed it "Bull Moose" after his self-perception of strength. Most would agree that's borderline pathetic. It's important to know when to quit!

Unfortunately, Teddy was also somewhat of a bigot and saw the white race as superior to others, which negatively impacted his policies around American imperialism and civil rights— a stain on an otherwise strong Presidency. But ultimately, Teddy soared. His spirit, vision, and powerful brand made America proud and strong. His broad agenda had a permanent, positive impact on our country.

Lessons in Leadership

Leaders who stand on conviction are rare. Teddy showed the conviction and the courage to address tough issues, even against powerful oppositional voices like the railroad industry. He focused on a few things with tenacity and passion to get things done, and he often worked with adversaries. He was a learner who loved to read and grow. He once said, "reading is a disease with me."

Teddy's brand was energy and authenticity. What you saw is what you got with Teddy—you never needed to guess! He brought a sense of excitement to the office. While not all leaders will create excitement, those whose energy is contagious can positively impact morale and improve the recruitment and retention of top talent. Teddy was a proud and confident man who used humor to defuse tension or drive home a point. A leader can be very self-assured yet occasionally use self-deprecation to become more relatable and ultimately admired.

One of the most challenging things for a leader is knowing when it's time to move on. Great leaders know when new talent is needed and take appropriate action. This was a miss for Teddy.

After leaving a job, it's also important to truly step away from the job and let the next person lead without the benefit of your outside opinion. Great leaders may seek the opinion of their predecessors, but unsolicited advice is rarely welcomed on any front.

A final leadership lesson Teddy demonstrated well was his ability to create balance in his life. He was committed to his family life and able to step away to restore himself when necessary. This leadership attribute is rarely opposed but frequently ignored.

CHAPTER 16

THE SPHINX

Franklin D. Roosevelt, 1933-1945

FRANKLIN D. ROOSEVELT (FDR), our 32nd president, was the right person at the right time in American history. In response to the ravages of the Great Depression and FDR's promise of a "new deal for the forgotten man," American voters overwhelmingly voted him into the presidency in 1932. This former governor of New York proved to be someone who would tackle tough issues. He not only led America out of the Great Depression with the New Deal, but he also positioned America as the dominant global power through World War II.

During his presidency, the public was granted a "safety net," and the federal government's role was dramatically changed. The series of domestic programs that constituted the New Deal stabilized the economy, provided jobs and relief for those who were suffering, and reformed the financial system. FDR's approach to his presidential power and his progressive agenda shifted the executive branch to the strongest of the three branches.

FDR's ability to communicate to the public, primarily with a series of radio addresses called fireside chats, was legendary. His vision of hope carried the country through some of its darkest hours. Like Abraham Lincoln, he used a challenging time to strengthen his focus on creating lasting change.

FDR looked to solve public issues with governmental solutions. He strengthened confidence in the banking system through the creation of the Federal Deposit Insurance Corporation (FDIC), established minimum wage and fair labor standards with the Fair Labor Standards Act (FLSA), distributed federal funds to state agencies for employment via the Federal Emergency Relief Act (FERA), reduced unemployment and improved U.S. infrastructure via the creation of the Public Works Administration (PWA), provided jobs and electricity to a seven-state area of the south by creating the Tennessee Valley Authority (TVA), and ensured financial support for the unemployed, disabled, and retired populations with the establishment of the Social Security Act (SSA). On the international front, FDR played a vital role in forming the United Nations.

Despite one's views on the role of government, it can't be argued that FDR's policies and programs helped millions during a very difficult time.

Lessons in Leadership

Great leaders have an essential responsibility to create trust. Those who focus on the needs of those they serve and consistently lead with integrity have an amazing opportunity to impact permanent change. FDR became the nation's leader during a very difficult time in our history and set a new permanent course for the country.

FDR created and maintained a powerful brand that allowed him to relate to both the suffering public and egotistical international leaders. He was from an aristocratic family, yet the most downtrodden citizens felt he could understand their issues. His communication skills were outstanding. His fireside chats facilitated a "cozy" community and created an opportunity to continually share vision, strategies, and tactics with his fellow Americans. During a particularly dark time in American history, he famously said "the only thing we have to fear is fear itself." This is an excellent example of how he inspired and rallied the country. If you want followership, communicate clearly and frequently.

My criticism of FDR is twofold: First, he broke the oath of Washington by running for a fourth term. This was later changed by law to prevent more than two terms, but FDR was dying and chose personal power over the country by running for another term. Second, despite being an excellent public communicator, FDR was a terrible internal communicator. He never told Harry Truman, his vice president and successor, about the atomic bomb, left him in the dark about war plans designed by Russia and England, and used a leadership method of pitting two people against each other to achieve the "best" outcome. This style of leadership may have short-term gains but, in the long run, creates distrust and uncertainty among peers.

Organizations need to think about the landscape and what type of leader they may need in a particular "season" of their business. Getting the right person at the right time in the right job is very important for stability and growth. The American public got it right with FDR. The voters chose him to lead through one of America's greatest times of uncertainty.

CHAPTER 17

THE SAGE OF MONTICELLO

Thomas Jefferson, 1801-1809

THOMAS JEFFERSON WAS A founding father and the 3rd president of the United States. He was a statesman and so much more: an architect, lawyer, horticulturist, educator, avid reader, and philosopher. Before his presidency, he held numerous elected or appointed positions, including delegate from Virginia to the Continental Congress, governor of Virginia, U.S. minister to France, secretary of state under George Washington, and vice president under John Adams.

Together with his colleagues, Jefferson studied Roman Law, the Magna Carta, and the governmental structures of England and France to create a vision and framework for building an experiment of government like none the world had ever seen. Jefferson was the principal author of the Declaration of Independence and was a major contributor to the writing of the U.S. Constitution.

As president, Jefferson was a visionary. He believed in limited government and was a strong supporter of states' rights. His view for the country's expansion was that of an agrarian society versus the industrial nation we became. He began the expansion of the continental United States with the Louisiana Purchase, which added 828,000 square miles and nearly doubled the size of the country. The present-day landmass of the United States and its position between oceans, ample supplies of fresh water, and large variety of land for agriculture makes us not only unique in the world, but it is one of the reasons we became and have stayed a world power for so long. Our position on the planet is nearly impossible to replicate.

Jefferson strongly supported education when it wasn't considered practical or necessary. He founded the University of Virginia, a renowned institution to this day. His foresight also led to the creation of West Point Academy.

Despite his brilliance, Jefferson had flaws. His opposition to a strong federal government, a national treasury, and the Embargo Act of 1807—which prohibited American ships from trading in all foreign ports—and his international isolationism all render a stain on the legacy of an otherwise outstanding leader.

Lessons in Leadership

If there was ever a president who epitomized being curious and upholding a desire to continue to learn, it was Thomas Jefferson. Jefferson had expertise in diverse areas such as science, agronomy, law, paleontology, entrepreneurship, and languages. He invented the macaroni maker and the pedometer, was fluent in six languages, and wrote the Declaration of Independence. During a meeting of dignitaries gathered at the White House, John Kennedy once said, "I think this is the most extraordinary collection of talent, of human knowledge, that has ever been gathered at the White House—with the possible exception of when Thomas Jefferson dined alone."

Relationships matter. Jefferson also built strong partnerships with key founding fathers and future presidents. He remained close and influential to this group through the formational stages of the country and throughout his life. He also formed a close relationship with a former competitor, John Adams. While that may not have impacted his presidency, I think it speaks to a leader's character when relationships are formed with former opponents.

Great leaders, however much they are respected, will have enemies. As previously mentioned, Jefferson had flaws, one being alienating those who disagreed with him. Alexander Hamilton, Treasury Secretary in George Washington's cabinet, was a frequent foe. Jefferson was quite selfish and threatened to resign his post as secretary of state in Washington's cabinet because he couldn't control Hamilton. Leadership roles often create jealousy among others, who often wish for leaders to fail. There will always be differences in opinion. Great leaders bring opponents close and try to find common ground.

While I'm not sure we mere mortals will ever master nearly what Jefferson did, we can all be curious, continue to learn, be interesting and interested, and benefit from the diverse, deep view of the world that results.

CHAPTER 18

GIVE 'EM HELL HARRY

Harry Truman, 1945-1953

HARRY TRUMAN WAS A family farmer, captain in the U.S. Army, county judge (without a law degree), small business owner, senator from Missouri, vice president, and ultimately the 33rd president of the United States. This trajectory wasn't unusual during this earlier period of U.S. history, but by 1944 the "rags to riches" presidential candidates were rare.

Truman was nominated to be President Franklin Roosevelt's running mate in 1944, during the last stages of World War II. While the inevitable conclusion to the war in Europe was becoming clear, the war in the Pacific looked like a very long road to travel. He had been vice president for just two months when FDR died.

Before he died, FDR had given Truman little to no information on post-war Europe plans that had been discussed and agreed to by Joseph Stalin and Winston Churchill. FDR also didn't tell Truman that the United States had completed testing on the atomic bomb, the nuclear weapon that not only changed the course of the second world war but also permanently changed the nature of global conflict.

Truman made the decision to drop atomic bombs on the Japanese cities of Hiroshima and Nagasaki in August 1945, which ended World War II. After the war, he pushed to rebuild both Germany and Japan, a remarkably smart and important strategy. History has shown that rebuilding and improving the lives of your enemies creates eventual allies. The Treaty of

Versailles, which ended World War I, was an example of what not to do. It was very punitive and harsh to Germany and ultimately led to the Second World War.

The creation and execution of the Marshall Plan, Truman's comprehensive program to rebuild Europe after World War II, saved lives, helped millions in need, and turned enemies into allies. Truman also created the Truman Doctrine, a pledge that the United States would provide political, military, and economic assistance to all democratic nations under threat from external or internal authoritarian forces. This doctrine led to U.S. involvement in Korea and later Vietnam. Like many policies, the Truman Doctrine is important to periodically review to validate its applicability to the present time. Not properly considering all the cause-and-effect elements can lead to such unintended consequences.

The Truman era also marked the beginning of the Cold War. He was behind the successful Berlin airlift of 1948, which essentially defied the USSR blockade around the city and represented the first major international crisis of the Cold War.

Truman came from humble roots and always had ordinary people in mind. He proposed health care for all to protect the poorest Americans. Although controversial at the point of introduction, the concept was socialized and generally accepted over time. Thanks to his work, Medicare became a reality in 1965 under Lyndon Johnson. Johnson signed the bill in front of Truman in 1965, and Truman became the first Medicare beneficiary. Nearly fifty-five years later, the Affordable Health Care law (a blueprint taken from Truman's vision) was passed.

Other notable Truman accomplishments that have had a lasting impact are ending segregation in the U.S. armed forces and forming of the North Atlantic Treaty Organization (NATO), National Security Council (NSC), the Central Intelligence Agency (CIA), National Security Agency (NSA), and the United Nations (UN).

On the downside, historians have a mixed view on Truman's decision to move forces into South Korea and the U.S. involvement in a war that ended in a stalemate. Truman relied on the recommendation of General McArthur's assessment of China's intentions of invading Korea and expanding communism. Coming off a world war and its devastation, it's no wonder one would want to do everything to prevent another major conflict.

Lessons in Leadership

Great leaders are courageous. Truman showed incredible courage as president. He was thrust into one of the most difficult positions imaginable regarding the use of the atomic bomb. The fact that he wasn't even aware of its existence gave him little time to sort out the global consequences. This decision involved far more than ending the war, it forever shaped the scope of how destructive humans could be. Truman took full responsibility for his actions as well as the actions of the government, epitomized with his famous "the buck stops here" philosophy. More leaders should similarly own their decisions and take responsibility for outcomes.

Truman also displayed outstanding focus and stayed true to his vision for the country. He accomplished or influenced several important doctrines, bills, and policies that still help Americans today. His vision, strategies, and tactics rarely wavered, even on occasions when they weren't popular. It's tempting to give in to popular demand rather than standing firm. Truman was willing even to lose reelection—and nearly did—to "stay the course."

Great leaders genuinely care for those they serve. Truman never lost sight of this principle. But despite his accomplishments, Truman was never that popular. While people saw him as honest, his brand was that of a "bullheaded man with a twangy voice." The lessons here are twofold: brand and communication skills. Harry didn't seem to care to improve either. Great leaders continue to grow and develop the core characteristics that guide them.

Leaders like Truman who are steadfast, not easily swayed by political powers, and dare to stand on their beliefs are a rare breed. Lincoln once said, "nearly all men can stand adversity. You want to see a man's character give them power." Truman demonstrated great character in the face of adverse times.

CHAPTER 19

IKE

Dwight D. Eisenhower, 1953-1961

GENERAL DWIGHT EISENHOWER (IKE) was Commander of the Allied Forces in World War II. His skill in navigating Allied interests and appeasing the British was worthy of its own medal. As a war hero, our nation's 34th president likely could have run on either party ticket and won!

Eisenhower was one of the presidents who inherited a perfect environment for domestic growth. Post-World War II expansion created jobs, education for veterans, and the unprecedented "baby boom." The U.S. had become the undisputed world power. It was a period unlike any other in American history. Ike benefitted from a robust economy, as he caught a tailwind of growth after World War II and expanded it.

Eisenhower ended the Korean war in 1953, mainly because enemy forces feared his military prowess. He also prevented conflicts from escalating into war on several occasions, primarily with the Soviet Union and later the Middle East.

The Eisenhower administration enacted the Federal-Aid Highway Act of 1956, which created the interstate highway system. This development had a tremendous impact on commerce, improved highway safety, and tied our country together from coast to coast. Ike also understood the interstate highway system's military value as a means for emergency evacuations, but his support for the project was still civilian in nature.

The federal budget was balanced three times under Eisenhower's leadership. His managerial skills were disciplined and built around accountability, much like his military skills.

Ike was also responsible for some disappointing actions. Not denouncing Senator Joseph McCarthy, who during the late 1940s and early 1950s promoted mostly unproven charges of communist subversion, was a mistake. He let a bully have an outsized influence that spread fear throughout the country. And while he promoted civil rights, Eisenhower wasn't a champion. Civil rights needed a champion.

The Cold War grew under Eisenhower's presidency. During this time the Soviet economy also expanded, as did the Arms race. But ultimately, Ike did keep America at peace through several potential confrontations, something America desperately needed at this point in history.

Lessons in Leadership

Great leaders focus on a few things that, if done well, make a difference. Eisenhower focused on details. His military approach to managing the presidency left little room for waste. Many leaders focus on too many unimpactful things—things that, even if accomplished, will have little impact on ultimate goals. Eisenhower organized and expended his energy around his vision for the country.

Ike was a classic example of the power of a brand. From leading the Allied forces during World War II to running the country and international affairs, his brand was so strong he avoided many of the hurdles and traps many before and after him faced. Since most of us are not five-star generals with international reputations, we need to be thoughtful about creating our brand and knowing why it is important. I have been amazed by how leaders have responded when asked what they thought their brand was and what they wanted it to be. For many, little thought had gone into it and, as a result, their brand was weak and ever-changing.

For all his earnest attention to detail, Ike occasionally used humor to make his points. He once quipped, "You don't lead by hitting people over the head—that's assault, not leadership!" A leader should always take responsibilities and important tasks seriously but not too seriously. That can lead to arrogance.

Great leaders lead balanced lives. Ike demonstrated this well. He was an outdoorsman who, during his presidency, liked to relax by fishing in the streams at Camp David. He was also an avid golfer. In fact, there is a tree at Augusta National Golf Club in Augusta, Georgia named after him. Not for what you would think—like a miracle shot off a branch—but because he frequently complained about the tree's location. What Ike didn't heed was his health. He did quit smoking in 1949 but later suffered four heart attacks and fourteen cardiac arrests. Too many leaders neglect their health because they are "too busy." It's easy to postpone medical exams or procrastinate on improvement goals around exercise and diet. Great leaders understand risk and reward. Ignoring your health is a loser's game.

CHAPTER 20

LBJ

Lyndon B. Johnson, 1963-1969

LYNDON JOHNSON WAS A teacher from Texas who rose to national prominence despite being seen as an outsider. First elected to the U.S. House of Representatives in 1937, Johnson's big personality and ability to get things done later led him to a leadership position in the Senate and ultimately the White House. He was elected vice president under President John F. Kennedy in 1960. He later took the oath of office himself, being sworn in as our nation's 36th president immediately following JFK's assassination in November 1963. In 1964, Johnson won the presidency in a landslide victory.

Johnson's accomplishments on the domestic front were impressive. He took a stalled civil rights bill—supported by Kennedy—and used his immense power from his days in Senate to pass The Civil Rights Act of 1964, which prohibited discrimination of the basis of race, color, religion, sex, or national origin. He enhanced immigration to allow more non-Europeans entry into the United States, giving the nation more diversity of color, thought, and values. He championed the "war on poverty," primarily through an ambitious series of domestic programs called "The Great Society." The main goals of this initiative were ending poverty, reducing crime, abolishing inequality, and improving the environment.

Laws that resulted from Johnson's "Great Society" reform package include Medicare, Medicaid, the Older Americans Act, the Elementary and

Secondary Education Act, and the Housing and Urban Development Act, all passed in 1965.

For all his accomplishments, Johnson was strangled by the Vietnam war. He lied about the Gulf of Tonkin incident, where the North Vietnamese fired on the USS Maddox, a mistruth that plunged the United States into Vietnam on a much larger scale. The unpopular war led to Johnson's depression and ultimately caused him to leave the office unceremoniously. Without the burden and mistakes of Vietnam, Johnson would have been remembered as a much better president than what his brand portrays.

Another failure was trying to push through both "guns and butter" (Vietnam and the Great Society agenda) at the same time. It created double-digit inflation and high unemployment. However, Johnson's legacy improves with time. For the most part, the positive impacts of the Great Society policies and programs outweigh his Vietnam failures.

Lessons in Leadership

Transformational change is not easy. Great leaders get big things done in the most efficient manner by crafting a clear vision to navigate a specific course. Lyndon Johnson demonstrated that exceptionally well with his "Great Society" agenda. He accomplished much by staying focused, leveraging relationships, establishing partnerships, and working with his opponents.

Great leaders can change and adapt. Johnson got to the root problems and made decisions that long needed to be addressed. His role in passing the Civil Rights Act—more than 100 years after the Emancipation Proclamation—and social safety net legislation (housing, Medicare, Medicaid, education) were courageous and overshadowed his racist history.

Great leaders recognize assets and leverage them. They typically have formed relationships they can call on when they need to create a win/win option. These relationships are not always corporate or legislative peers.

Johnson's wife, Lady Bird, was very smart and popular. He was wise always to have her at his side.

Unfortunately, the stress the presidency and Vietnam war had on Johnson led to a very unbalanced and unhealthy mental state. His depression not only hurt his brand but also harmed his health. Most of the time when we don't believe we can afford to rest is when we absolutely need it most. Great leaders understand that and religiously practice self-care.

CHAPTER 21

THE SCHOOLMASTER

Woodrow Wilson, 1913-1921

WOODROW WILSON WAS A two-term president who led the United States through World War I. Known as a progressive who shaped U.S. diplomacy through U.S. economic values, prior to becoming our 28th president, he was a lawyer, college professor, president of Princeton University, and governor of New Jersey.

Wilson was a reserved man who was incredibly confident in his vision for America. "Wilsonianism," his foreign policy that advocated for democracy and capitalism, would shape the United States' foreign policy throughout the 1900s. He moved America away from isolationism, which had generally guided the previous presidents, to internationalism. He was fiercely against imperialism, though, and moved to influence other nations into moral democracy, a system that only supports countries with similar ideologies.

After World War I, Wilson was the leading architect of the League of Nations, an intergovernmental organization designed to arbitrate international disputes and prevent future wars. He won the Nobel Prize in 1920 for his leadership in the Treaty of Versailles, which outlined the terms of surrender and included the charter for the League of Nations. While Wilson's plans to end World War I and create the League of Nations were embraced by the Allies, his failure to engage Congress resulted in their failure to enact the bill. Ultimately the League failed because it didn't include major powers defeated in World War I and didn't get U.S. support. It did lay the groundwork for two important lasting actions: the formation of the United Nations and the collective effort of nations to help with humanitarian needs across the globe.

Wilson was also progressive in U.S. domestic policy. Under his leadership, the country experienced the most comprehensive federal oversight of the nation's economy up to that time. He established the Federal Reserve, reduced tariffs, created more federal regulation of business, supported collective bargaining, and promoted labor over industry. He also created significant aid for agriculture and education during his terms in office.

Wilson's leadership shifted the Democratic party from that of the common man to the party of reform. In 1914, he enacted the Federal Trade Commission to protect consumers and promote competition. He signed the Adamson Act, which established an eight-hour workday with additional pay for overtime work for railroad workers.

Although initially reluctant, Wilson advocated for and signed the 19th Amendment giving women the right to vote—finally! One hundred and forty-four years after the Declaration of Independence famously proclaimed, "We hold these truths to be self-evident, that all men are created equal, that they are endowed by their creator with certain unalienable rights, that among these are life, liberty, and the pursuit of happiness," women finally got to participate in their governance.

Wilson's impact on our nation was profound. But despite his significant accomplishments, several decisions and policies attributed to him had severe, long-lasting adverse effects on our country and the world. First was his uncompromising support of the Treaty of Versailles. The treaty ended World War I and demanded Germany to pay nearly 33 billion dollars in reparations. This left Germany in ruins and ultimately gave rise to Hitler's Nazism and the brutally destructive World War II. Wilson's distrust of socialism and contempt for Russia led to the Cold War and the U.S.-Soviet Arms Race. While he was not solely responsible, all conflicts begin with the creation of an enemy, and Wilson planted the seed when Russia's communism was just starting.

Wilson also diluted civil rights and erased some advances made for African Americans during the Reconstruction era. He promoted Jim Crow laws, supported white-only buildings, dining, hotels, etc. And not only did he support segregation, but also supported the re-segregation of multiple federal government agencies, including the Treasury, Post Office, Navy, and the War Department.

Lessons in Leadership

Wilson demonstrated courage, challenged industry, and defended the worker. Many leaders don't have the stomach to stand up to money and influence. Wilson did, and not just with one or two acts or policies, but an entire agenda to change the government's role in our country. Wilson was a steadfast visionary, especially in developing and maintaining a roadmap for world peace.

Great leaders are great communicators. Wilson was a leader who continually worked on his communication skills. He overcame dyslexia and used persuasion as a powerful tool to achieve his ambitious agenda.

Leaders can learn as much from the flaws and mistakes of others as they can from examples of success. Wilson had the flaw of trying to do too much himself. He excluded his allies from the process of negotiating the Treaty of Versailles. If a leader needs others to support a cause, project, or strategy, they need to bring others along in the process. Not all decisions need to go to vote, but those requiring followership should include participation and buy-in. The same "go it alone" strategy also cost Wilson when the U.S. Congress would not support the League of Nations.

Great leaders build and support talent—people who can provide expertise and opinion to complete the challenges leaders face. Wilson seemed to think he was always the smartest guy in the room, a prevalent and "deadly" characteristic of leaders who don't listen to others or surround themselves with such talent. Going at it alone is rarely a winning strategy.

CHAPTER 22

THE ERA OF GOOD FEELINGS PRESIDENT

James Monroe, 1817-1825

JAMES MONROE WAS THE last of our nation's "founding fathers" who served as president. Monroe, the 5th U.S. president, was a quality leader whose accomplishments exceeded his failures. During his two terms, Monroe continued to expand the country—adding the states of Mississippi, Illinois, Alabama, Maine, and Missouri—and neutralized conflict in the Great Lakes and Florida.

Monroe's presidency is mainly noted for his international positioning of the United States in what became known as the Monroe Doctrine. This doctrine put the world on notice that the United States would not interfere with European affairs but warned that any further colonization, expansion, or interference in the Western Hemisphere would be viewed as a potentially hostile act. This doctrine is the backbone of U.S. foreign policy to this day.

Monroe was a charming, warm, and compromising leader. He ushered in what came to be known as the "Era of Good Feeling," reflecting Monroe's personal style. He was an influence on the government, but not one who needed to be the force of government.

The missed opportunity of Monroe's presidency was his failure to secure a cooperative agreement with Great Britain to end the slave trade in 1815 with the Treaty of Ghent. This agreement would have had a significant impact on the United States and around the world. To Monroe's credit, in his State of the Union address in 1824, he called that failing out as a great regret. The agreement's language had no teeth, only faith that justice would prevail over profit.

In hindsight, Monroe had an opportunity to set a new course that could have changed history. The issue of partisanship, while small, began to establish a precedent. As a founder, he foresaw the dangers of partisanship and called it out early as a threat to our form of government.

Lessons in Leadership

James Monroe's leadership style of charm, warmth, and desire to compromise is not typically on the list of successful traits of strong leaders. I would argue it is on the list of strong people. Strength is often misjudged and interpreted as harsh. Followership and impact are far more guided by trust, respect, and listening skills. Monroe's attributes are honorable and noble. I would much rather be known as warm and willing to listen and compromise than thick-headed and prideful. Arrogant and prideful leaders may experience short-term gains, but typically have fewer allies and friends when their duties end. You can and should be both strong and have genuine humbleness.

Great leaders deal with an issue's root cause before it becomes a major problem. This is a crucial leadership trait. Very rarely does a problem become overwhelming "out of the blue." It is typically something we are aware of, often for long periods. Most leaders tend to address the symptoms rather than the root cause because the latter typically carries pain and unpopularity. Not dealing with the issue of slavery was a big miss for Monroe.

The moral of the story is to continuously address problems at the root. If you see something that doesn't seem right, it probably isn't! Stand by those who are wronged or most vulnerable. It's what great leaders do. It's what great people do, too.

CHAPTER 23
YOUNG HICKORY
James K. Polk, 1845-1849

JAMES POLK, KNOWN AS "Young Hickory," was a protégé of Andrew Jackson. Like Jackson, he was an incredible and strong-willed orator who was focused on communicating and executing his plans. During his presidency, America's territory grew by more than one-third, extending across the continent for the first time.

Our 11th president was a dark horse candidate in the 1844 presidential race. His resume included serving in the Tennessee legislature, U.S. House of Representatives, and governor of Tennessee, yet he remained relatively unknown outside local political circles. Polk was a known workaholic whose ambitious agenda included a four-part promise that he accomplished after only four years. Despite being very popular, he then stepped down from office.

This was an era where manifest destiny—"America's right to the land we now occupy"—first became a focus. Polk led the nation through the Mexican-American War, gaining territory including Texas, New Mexico, California, Nevada, Utah, most of Arizona, Colorado, and parts of Oklahoma, Kansas, and Wyoming. He reduced tariffs, which made America's products more competitive with world trade. He reformed the national banking system by creating an independent U.S. Treasury Department as opposed to using state or private banks for federal reserve, and he settled a boundary dispute with Great Britain that secured the

Oregon Territory for the United States. Polk also established the U.S. Naval Academy, the Smithsonian Institute, and the Department of the Interior.

Despite his accomplishments, Polk's aggressive acquisition of land reignited the slavery debate, which ultimately led to civil war in the 1860s. While acquiring land through war may have significantly benefitted the United States' goal of expansion, it is viewed quite differently by Mexico and Spain, the countries we fought for the land. One must ask if the ends justify the means.

Lessons in Leadership

Great leaders are true to their mission and word. Polk did what he said he was going to do. Then, unlike most leaders and politicians, he stepped away from his power after achieving his goals.

Polk focused on a few things and did them well. He was highly focused and clear on his priorities, what was important and how to get them done. Like all great leaders, he achieved this by being courageous and an influential communicator. The priorities he had were high stakes, and he went for it.

Many leaders have pet projects or views of what is important and put their energy toward them at the expense of fundamental issues that would have an even more significant future impact. Polk's leadership failure was not trying to resolve the slavery issue with the new territory and his popularity. Maybe that's why he stepped down, or perhaps it wasn't something he felt needed to be done at that time. But it wasn't an obscure issue, so it appears he dodged the root problem facing the country. Short-sightedness can be as big a problem as not getting your priorities done.

CHAPTER 24

JACK

John F. Kennedy, 1961-1963

IN 1961 JOHN F. Kennedy (JFK) became the 35th president of the United States, the first Roman Catholic, and our youngest elected president. An inspiring leader, he was born into a wealthy family and married to a beautiful young socialite. JFK's youthful appearance and relaxed, confident style ushered in a new period of optimism and infatuation with the first family—which included two small children—on both the U.S. and world stages. Before occupying the White House, Kennedy was a war hero, congressman, and author. His best-selling book of short biographies, *Profiles in Courage*, won a Pulitzer Prize in 1957.

Kennedy's political style was that of a moderate reformer. For example, he used a Republican strategy of lowering taxes to bring the United States out of a recession and leaned heavily into social reform in what he called "The New Frontier." His domestic policy achievements included expanded unemployment benefits, improved housing, anti-poverty programs and increased minimum wage. He also led comprehensive legislation to help farmers with the Agricultural Act of 1961.

Kennedy laid the groundwork for the Civil Rights Bill of 1964 that Johnson later passed. While he recognized civil rights as a moral cause and signed executive orders around affirmative action, he didn't advance the issue as far as his political capital may have allowed him to. He was hesitant because it wasn't politically safe to do so.

Under Kennedy's leadership, international accomplishments were impressive. He reformed immigration by advocating for the elimination of discriminatory "national origins" quotas. He created the Peace Corps, a new agency that provided an opportunity for Americans to voluntarily serve at home and abroad with the mission to "promote world peace and friendship." The Peace Corp positively impacted the worldview many nations hold toward the United States to this day.

Confrontations with the USSR (Soviet Union) marked Kennedy's presidency: first, the Bay of Pigs Invasion in 1961, a failed landing operation on the southwestern coast of Cuba conducted by Cuban exiles against leader Fidel Castro and covertly financed by the U.S. government; and later the Cuban Missile Crisis, a 1962 confrontation between the United States and the Soviet Union around missile placements in Italy and Turkey for the U.S. and Cuba for the Soviet Union, which achieved peaceful resolution.

Given the Soviet Union's strength, Kennedy masterfully balanced the power struggle between the two nations. While the formation of the Partial Nuclear Test Ban Treaty may not seem monumental given its amendments to and ultimate failure, it established a standard of how the world "should" control nuclear weapons.

The conflict in Vietnam proved problematic for Kennedy. He expanded U.S. presence there with both Special Forces troops and military advisors, in effect lighting the fire in what has proven to be one of America's worst political wars and failures.

John F. Kennedy was assassinated on November 22, 1963, as he rode in a motorcade through downtown Dallas. The death of this popular, charismatic president had a profound impact on the country and our view of his accomplishments and failures. One can't help but wonder what might have happened with Vietnam, civil rights legislation and international affairs had he lived to serve another term. While tragedy tends to inflate our view of "lives cut short," time also allows us to look closer at a person's character. For all his potential and charm, JFK's womanizing and questionable personal relationships outside of official White House business are a dark blemish on this young president's legacy.

Lessons in Leadership

Communication, communication, communication. Remember that leadership is a speaking role, and JFK was a strong inspirational public speaker who used charm and confidence to establish his iconic brand. This charismatic young man came to the national stage just when televisions were moving from a luxury to a staple item in nearly all the American living rooms. His optimistic and aspirational speeches included inspiring quotes that are widely repeated yet today.

Great leaders understand the importance of followership. Whether building sustainable partnerships or building a team, you don't need to always have your way. Leaders who know that you don't have to make every issue a "must-win" but can play the long game create more allies and fewer enemies. Kennedy was very clever with how he created and executed his priorities. He lowered taxes, typically not a Democratic approach, and then moved heavily into social programs. Everybody felt like they had won something.

Kennedy also demonstrated courage when the country needed it most during the highest-stakes game—nuclear war. The ability to "own" the difficult decision, knowing failure would be tragic, is something most pass on. Kennedy didn't blink. What was disappointing, though, was that he did blink on issues of lesser stake if there was potential to hurt his political standing. His failure to address the Civil Rights movement of the day would be an example.

Every leader should understand the importance of not abusing their power and authority. JFK was a known womanizer who took advantage of his status. Unfortunately, he was protected by the same media that protected his father, also known for similar behaviors. It is unlikely JFK could get away with this today. We may not be a more moral society in the 21st century, but today there are countless forms of media and unprecedented opportunities to expose a leader's failings. (At least in theory.)

CHAPTER 25

Takeaways on the Top Twelve

AS VIEWED THROUGH THE lens of leadership, these top presidents, leading in diverse periods of American history, all made us better as a country. Their styles, backgrounds, platforms, and popularity at the time differed. But they had common traits that gave us a common thread. They were all long-term thinkers who had a core vision for the country. They were humbled by the office and inspirational at the same time. They felt a strong sense of stewardship and responsibility to serve the country. They earned followership. They were burdened with the demands of the office, which reflects how much responsibility they felt the role held. They made mistakes, fought political divides, faced crises, and avoided even more. They demonstrated a driving conviction to their vision and how to best lead our country. And history has shown, for the most part, they were right.

These twelve presidents stood out for their courage yet had their shortcomings. Many led our country during challenging times. I often wondered while reading their biographies how they would have done at other times. Was the best made for the times, or by the times? I believe most, if not all, would have been outstanding at any time in history.

Without crucial events, many of these leaders would not be remembered as favorably. I doubt capitals or buildings would have been named for Lincoln or FDR without their powerful examples of endurance through extremely difficult times. But crises are not foundational to greatness. Without headwinds, I believe they would have demonstrated their greatness in other ways. Ways that would have similarly made our country better.

PART THREE

The Bottom U.S. Presidents

Through the Lens of Leadership

CHAPTER 26

Thoughts on the Bottom Twelve

WHILE OUR TOP PRESIDENTS have been reviewed, debated, and memorialized by historians for many years, our worst presidents haven't been scrutinized as formally. In 1948, preeminent historian Arthur Schlesinger asked fifty-five historians how they rated the American presidents. Schlesinger asked historians to place each president (except William Henry Harrison and James Garfield because of short terms) into six categories: great, near-great, high average, average, below average, and failure. It was assumed the scholars were to decide for themselves what was greatness and what was failure. The review criteria included rating "ones who failed to safeguard us and adequately lead us during periods of crisis or tainted the office through scandal and incompetence." Since this earliest poll, credible organizations such as US News & World Report, Siena College Research Institute, and C-SPAN Presidential Historians have conducted numerous surveys. The bottom "usual suspects" of James Buchanan, Andrew Johnson, and Warren Harding consistently appear. These presidents are not only considered in the "failure" category, but historical opinions of them haven't seemed to change over time.

To thoroughly analyze the impact of a leader, you need to evaluate the quality, sustainability, and impact of their programs and policies over an extended period. Several presidents' "stock values" have either increased or decreased historically as we look at the impact of their programs or behaviors within the changing societal norms. An example of this is John F. Kennedy—a bright young leader whose life was cut short in office and who was immediately classified as one of our best presidents. This is not an argument against the polling or historians' views, but rather a reminder that JFK was a womanizer. Considering the women's rights initiatives that followed in the late twenty-first century and the more recent "Me Too" movements, this unsavory behavior impacts his position today. On the flip side, time has a way of healing past doings. Ulysses S. Grant's administration was embroiled in controversy and scandals. After his presidency, many historians branded him one of our nation's most corrupt presidents. Over time, though, several historians have painted a different picture of a president who knit together a frayed union, lifted formerly enslaved people, and was far more humane with Native American policies.

In some ways, it feels unfair to judge or rank the least impactful presidents of the United States. They were all intelligent and had a desire to serve our country. However, the presidential office holds less power to execute strategies than most realize. While the president sets the agenda for the country and leads their political party, they have far less authority than a corporate CEO. The corporate CEO reports to a board of directors and its shareholders but is rarely confined by the board to enact policies and programs. The U.S. Constitution intentionally made the Executive office the weakest of the three branches of government. At the time, there was much concern that the president would simply be a replacement for the monarchy we had recently left. Even after Washington unselfishly stepped away from the office, the fear of one person being an unchecked power dictated how acceptable norms were established.

Throughout American history, the public has demanded either more federal influence (FDR is an example) or wanted less federal, centralized control. In a country built "...of the people, by the people, for the people," promoting the rights of its citizens and specifically stating that we have inalienable rights of life, liberty, and the pursuit of happiness, it is evident that many of our presidents failed to represent the peoples' best interests of the time. Either their own biases or the ability to press Congress caused many to "punt" issues to the next president. This is terrible leadership, something I will use to demonstrate why these men are perceived as failures and largely forgotten.

Great leaders surround themselves with the best people. People who tell the truth and execute according to the agreed-upon plan. The team grows together and is committed to the greater good as opposed to self-interest. Many leaders start with good intentions, but either get lazy or prideful. When they act outside of policies, laws, or standards, they are forever impacting those they lead and serve. I have given presidents a harsher judgment if they knew what they were doing was wrong and tried to circumvent or create their own rules. I was more lenient with presidents who were somewhat incompetent or overly trusting of others but not unethical.

Bottom Twelve Presidents Ranked Through the Lens of Leadership

30. Zachary Taylor	1849-1850, Whig, elected for one term, died in office, 12th president
31. Rutherford B. Hayes	1877-1881, Republican, elected for one term, 19th president
32. Martin Van Buren	1837-1841, Democrat, elected for one term, 8th president
33. Richard Nixon	1969-1974, Republican, elected for two terms, resigned in office, 37th president
34. Herbert Hoover	1929-1933, Republican, elected for one term, 31st president
35. Millard Fillmore	1850-1853, Know Nothing/Whig, non-elected, filled in after Zachary Taylor's death, 13th president
36. Chester Arthur	1881-1885, Republican, elected for one term, 21st president
37. John Tyler	1841-1845, Whig, non-elected, filled in after William Henry Harrison's death, 10th president
38. Warren Harding	1921-1923, Republican, elected for one term, died in office, 29th president
39. Franklin Pierce	1853-1857, New Hampshire Democratic Party, elected for one term, 14th president
40. Andrew Johnson	1865-1869, Republican, non-elected: filled in after Abraham Lincoln's assassination, 17th president
41. James Buchanan	1857-1861, Democratic Party, elected for one term, 15th president

CHAPTER 27

TEN CENT JIMMY

James Buchanan, 1857-1861

JAMES BUCHANAN WAS RATED by many historians as the most-inept president in U.S. history. Our 15th president was tarnished with that dubious honor primarily because he took no action to unite a country sharply divided over the issue of slavery and did nothing to stop Southern states from seceding. He solidified this bottom spot with his support for the Dred Scott Decision, in which the United States Supreme Court ruled that enslaved people were the legal property of their owners, Congress had no power to prevent the spread of slavery, and that African American people were not U.S. citizens and never would be. Thinking his support of Dred Scott would put the slave issue to rest, it did just the opposite.

Buchanan surrounded himself with like-minded others. His cabinet members were sympathetic to and supportive of the South, including the Secretary of War, John B. Floyd, who would later become a general in the Confederate States Army.

Prior to the civil war, few presidents did much to address slavery, and few did much to accelerate civil rights after the war. So why are scholars and historians so hard on Buchanan? Partly because he was arguably the most prepared for the role of Chief Executive. He had more experience and preparation for the role than perhaps any president before him. He was a successful lawyer who served in the Pennsylvania State legislature and the U.S. Senate and House of Representatives. He was secretary of state and an ambassador to Russia and Great Britain. Unfortunately, his experience did not translate into leadership. Despite his impressive resume, he failed to act and demonstrated he was overwhelmed with the responsibilities of the presidency. His successor, Abraham Lincoln, was arguably the least prepared candidate with a small law practice, a short stint in the Illinois House of Representatives, and one term in the U.S. House of Representatives. History has been much kinder to Abe and rightfully so!

Lessons in Leadership

Leadership requires courage, something James Buchanan lacked. He seemed to purposely support only the interests and philosophies of the Confederate south. Regardless of a person's personal perspectives, the president of the United States is first and foremost supposed to defend and protect the Constitution and the Union itself. If he felt the way he did—which he had the personal right to—he shouldn't have run for president of the United States. I can't imagine too many leaders purposely leading an effort to destroy versus protect what they have been elected or called to lead.

Buchanan surrounded himself with yes-men, something weak leaders do. As a result, he was never challenged and became emboldened to continue the divisive path he was on. This is a real challenge for any administration or organization. Many leaders don't want to be disagreed with or hear bad news. Having a culture that encourages constructive feedback and opinions is critical. Leaders who are insecure or have an inflated ego struggle with this the most. An environment that encourages vigorous discourse leads to better outcomes and reduces the risk of serious mistakes.

It's important to note that experience or education doesn't dictate leadership success. There is little correlation between where a person studies and how a person learns when it comes to leadership skills. That is not to say experience and education aren't important but having a lot of either doesn't guarantee success. I see education and experience to be a lifelong journey. As a student of life and leadership, I love the thought of constantly striving to learn. The more you understand, the less judgmental you become; the more you can relate and appreciate the differences and needs of others, the more you can truly lead.

CHAPTER 28

THE TENNESSEE TAILOR

Andrew Johnson, 1865-1869

ANDREW JOHNSON BECAME OUR nation's 17th president after Lincoln was assassinated in the days that immediately followed the end of the Civil War. A Tennessee Democrat, he was chosen as Republican Abraham Lincoln's running mate in the 1864 election. Johnson's path to the presidency was via the Tennessee legislature, U.S. Congress, governor of Tennessee, and vice presidency.

Lincoln chose Johnson as vice president to help with the impending reconstruction after the civil war. Johnson, a former tailor, related to the common person. He wasn't formally educated yet was known to have memorized the United States Constitution. He was reportedly drunk at Lincoln's inauguration, just five weeks before Lincoln's assassination and becoming president himself. Clearly not a good start on the national stage!

Johnson's most significant errors occurred around two key vetoes: First against The Freedman's Bureau Bill and later the Civil Rights Act of 1866, each designed to establish rights for African people born in or brought into the United States as enslaved people. Both vetoes were ultimately overridden, and the legislation enacted. Given Johnson's unpopularity in Congress, including among members of his own party, the Reconstruction Act of 1867 was passed over his veto as well. On May 29, 1865, after the American Civil War had ended, Johnson issued sweeping pardons to thousands of former Confederate officers and soldiers. Granting a pardon is an executive order considered "a means of forgiveness of a president after an individual has shown that they have accepted responsibility for their crime as part of their pardon process." This move proved to be very controversial in the Northern states.[3]

The country needed to wait out Johnson's term to address Black suffrage and the passage of the Fifteenth Amendment, which forbid denial of voting based on "race, color, or previous condition of servitude." Johnson chose not to run for reelection in 1868, then followed with several failed attempts to get back to Washington as a Tennessee senator or representative.

Lastly, Andrew Johnson was impeached after he breached the Tenure of Office Act in 1867. This act was intended to restrict the president's power to remove certain office holders without the approval of the Senate. Johnson had recently removed Edwin Stanton, Secretary of War, which brought about the impeachment trial. He survived removal from office by just one vote. (In 1926, in the case of Myers v. the United States, a Supreme Court ruling held that presidents did in fact have the power to remove officials from office.) While Johnson was ultimately vindicated, his legacy remains that of the first president ever impeached.

Lessons in Leadership

One of the greatest harms to an organization or a country is to keep an incompetent leader in their role. It is critical to properly vet and understand a leader before placing them in a position of responsibility. As a candidate, Johnson wasn't vetted beyond where he lived: in Tennessee, a southern state that would presumably help reconstruct the South after the civil war. He was a bad pick.

Great leaders establish and maintain followership. One of several distinguishing characteristics of President Johnson was he never really

---

3 "President Andrew Johnson Pardons Confederate John C. Shelton, 1866," *Document Bank of Virginia,* accessed June 23, 2022, https://edu.lva.virginia.gov/dbva/items/show/149.

warmed to the position, and the American people never seemed to warm to him.

Too many people aspire to a leadership role for money or power. A true understanding of why they want to serve should underpin the heart of a leader. Managers are replaceable. Great leaders are different. They lead not for themselves but rather a purpose greater than themselves. They coach their team and develop them. They manage to a vision, strategy, and tactics of an organizational plan. They inspire others to follow. Johnson failed all these key competencies.

CHAPTER 29
HANDSOME FRANK
Franklin Pierce, 1853-1857

FRANKLIN PIERCE WAS VIEWED as a northerner who could bridge southern interests, making him a good compromise for the Democrats in 1852. Prior to becoming our nation's 14th president, he was a lawyer who served in the New Hampshire legislature and went on to win election to two terms in the U.S. House of Representatives and one in the Senate. He was known for being outgoing, popular, and quite good-looking.

Pierce believed that abolitionism was a threat to the country. To protect his popularity, he tried to have it both ways, though. He claimed to detest slavery, yet appeased slavery supporters by backing the Kansas-Nebraska act, a law that allowed residents in these territories to decide whether they would allow slavery. He also enforced the Fugitive Slave Acts, laws passed in 1793 and 1850 to provide the return of enslaved people who escaped from one state into another state or territory.

To his credit, Pierce authorized the purchase of a sizable amount of land that later became part of Arizona and New Mexico. This purchase provided the land necessary for a southern transcontinental railroad and resolved conflicts that lingered after the Mexican-American war.

Pierce's leadership skills and style were largely ineffective. He was viewed as a contrarian, primarily by his own party. He suffered personal heartaches. Three of his sons died before adulthood, and his wife was frequently ill and suffered from depression. He was a heavy drinker who ultimately died from cirrhosis of the liver in 1869.

Pierce served just one term as president. To his disappointment, the Democrats abandoned him by refusing to renominate him in 1856. In response, he became a persistent critic of President Lincoln during the civil war.

Lessons in Leadership

One of the best bits of advice I got when preparing for retirement from a forty-year professional career was "don't walk the hallways." Aside from mentees or an occasional former colleague seeking advice, it's best to leave your presence and opinions away from your former workplace. Honestly, it's egotistical to think others want to continue to hear your thoughts and opinions. Franklin Pierce provided a lot of unsolicited advice in the years following his presidency, which further deteriorated an already tarnished brand. Leaving gracefully is an art. While we'd all like to leave "on top," not all have that privilege. How one exits and moves forward has a significant impact on the organization they leave and one's legacy. Trying to boost your legacy post-service is challenging, and it rarely benefits the person or those they lead.

Decision-making is a critical leadership skill. Some decisions are based on best-available information and what the leader thinks is in the best interest of those they serve. While maybe later proven wrong, decisions made with wise counsel and good intent should be respected. You're never going to please everyone. Pierce is a classic example of trying to play both sides and failing miserably. If your goal is to be popular, don't be a leader! If your goal is to be an effective leader, evaluate options, seek counsel, measure possible outcomes, and make good decisions. People are counting on it.

CHAPTER 30

WOBBLY WARREN

Warren Harding, 1921-1923

WARREN HARDING, OUR 29TH president, famously summed up his own presidency by saying, "I am not fit for this office and never should have been here." At least he was honest about his leadership! Harding was a successful newspaper publisher, which gave him an avenue to promote himself into the office. He was also a former state senator and lieutenant governor of Ohio before rising to the U.S. presidency.

Harding rose to power because he was a good communicator who played into the theme of "getting back to normal" after the disruptions of World War I, a worldwide pandemic (Spanish Flu), and tight business regulations associated with the Wilson administration. And frankly, as one of his Ohio promoters noted, he "looked like a president." He was noted for his affability and strong desire to please; unfortunately, he was also known as an unrestrained womanizer. His office was filled with self-dealing and corruption. His appointees and cronies plundered the U.S. government, including the infamous "Teapot Dome" where Harding's Secretary of the Interior, Albert Fall, was bribed by oilmen to tap into government oil reserves. Fell was convicted of the crime and became the first cabinet member in history to serve prison time.

Despite his generally inept administration, Harding did sign the Budget and Accounting Act of 1921, which established the country's first formal budgeting process and created the Bureau of the Budget.

Harding died of a heart attack after less than thirty months in office. After his death, scandals and affairs came to light, further diminishing his popularity and brief presidency.

Lessons in Leadership

We learn a lot about leadership quality after a leader has left. Was their work sustainable, or was it "smoke and mirrors?" As it turns out, Warren Harding was not just corrupt but in over his head. He didn't pay attention to his cabinet members' dealings and tried to play both sides on the hottest issues of the day.

Harding was an eleventh-hour backroom decision as a candidate, primarily based upon a brand he had established as a publisher. Picking leaders based on appearance is usually a big mistake. This typically occurs because there hasn't been much work done around leadership development. The tendency is to default to form over substance.

I had the privilege of co-creating and leading a leadership development program at my former place of employment. It was designed by leaders for leaders, with a focus on small-group interaction and sharing core leadership, coaching, and management principles. This allowed emerging leaders to observe and learn from other leaders. Leadership development is typically an under-resourced business. Done well, it can be one of the most important investments you make in your leaders and your organization's future. It gives others not only a deeper understanding of the depth of your leadership bench but best prepares you to avoid last-minute, smoky backroom disasters.

CHAPTER 31

HIS ACCIDENCY

John Tyler, 1841-1845

JOHN TYLER WAS AN unexpected and to many an "accidental" president. A former vice president, Tyler became our nation's 10th president after President William Henry Harrison died unexpectedly after just 31 days in office.

In the 1840 election, Tyler joined the William Henry Harrison ticket as part of a young party, the Whigs. Tyler had previously been a member of the U.S. House of Representatives, governor of Virginia, and U.S. senator. He was an avid slavery advocate and strongly believed in states' rights. Once Tyler became president, he opposed everything his adopted party stood for. Harrison, his predecessor, had just named his cabinet when Tyler took over. Most of the cabinet resigned, and he was expelled from the Whig party.

While Tyler's time in office was unremarkable, he did annex Texas in 1884, and under his leadership, the first telegraph line was completed between Baltimore and Washington D.C. Both events had a positive impact on our country.

After failing to receive the Whig's endorsement, Tyler launched a third-party bid for the presidency and lost. After leaving office, he joined the Confederacy and was elected to the Confederate South Senate. Tyler proved to not only turn on his party but his country. What a legacy!

Lessons in Leadership

Great leaders are aligned to the mission and vision of the organization they serve. Tyler wasn't vetted well in terms of aligning with his party. Many organizations spend significant time with succession planning but very little time probing into how a leader will align with what the organization needs at the time. Tyler was also not one to compromise, which is a critical leadership skill. There is no followership without common ground.

During my own leadership journey, I came to realize how important it was to evaluate talent and align the leader with the marketplace they would serve. What characteristics, strengths, and style are most needed for this group at this time? Any leader can create a strategy and implement change. The most sustainable results come when people understand and want to follow. This comes by aligning and relating to your team.

I had the privilege of building out an entire leadership team across the country. Each region had its unique challenges and opportunities. Since not all the regional positions became available simultaneously, it required that we (I sought counsel from trusted advisors) placed leaders from our talented team first on the needs of the market and then on the best fit. By not simply selecting the next person in line we created a significant sustainable impact.

The Whigs had no business putting Tyler on the ticket. Tyler saw slave-owner rights as his priority, while much of the country was turning against the issue by this time. Many leaders are placed in a position by looking through a rear-view mirror rather than to what is needed for the future. Tyler was a clear demonstration of this.

CHAPTER 32
GENTLEMAN BOSS
Chester Arthur, 1881-1885

CHESTER ARTHUR WAS ONE of the few United States presidents who wasn't actually elected to office. He became our 21st president after the assassination of his predecessor, James Garfield, in 1881.

Prior to becoming vice president, Arthur was a schoolteacher and lawyer. He also held the position of Head of Customs. This was a very lucrative and influential role at the time. After becoming president, he not only filled but overstaffed the Customs office with personal relationships and friends of the party. That in and of itself isn't unusual. What was unusual was his change of heart once "he got his." In what was known as the Pendleton Civil Service Reform Act, after he and his friends greatly benefitted from the Customs department, he reformed it so no one else could. The Pendleton Act alone wasn't what caused the public and Congress to lose faith and trust in Arthur. It did, however, lead to ongoing questioning of his honesty.

The first general federal immigration laws were enacted under Arthur's leadership. This law excluded "paupers, criminals, and lunatics" from coming to the United States. These were probably socially accepted terms of the day, but one must wonder what criteria was for judging some as a "lunatic." (It would be interesting to overlay the definition to some of our politicians, faith leaders, and media personalities today!) Unfortunately, there was tremendous discrimination against the Chinese during this era, and Arthur placed a 10-year suspension on immigration for people from China.

Arthur's presidential style was very deliberate and analytical. He was known to be a self-critical workaholic. His reputation became one of hypocrisy, intolerance, authoritativeness, and impatience. Because he had lost trust from his allies early on, this became an obstacle to gaining support for his agenda. As a result, he was forced to act independently, and leadership requires cooperation.

Arthur made a half-hearted effort to become the Republican presidential nominee in 1884 but did not have the party's support. He wisely chose not to push for what would have been an inevitable disappointment.

Lessons in Leadership

A leader must be someone you can trust. You don't always have to agree, and you may not have a say in many things that impact you, but we should be able to trust those in authority. I've found most leaders you can't trust are usually serving themselves and getting ahead at any expense. I've also learned most of those who can't trust others can't be trusted themselves. Quite simply, leaders who can't be trusted don't belong in leadership. Chester Arthur probably never belonged in the White House based on this basic principle.

Cronyism is never acceptable. Neither is nepotism, or any other form of unearned favoritism. That's not to say you don't surround yourself with people you know personally who are talented and trustworthy. Knowing who will get the job done and have your back is valuable. That's very different from filling positions or otherwise putting people in roles who are your buddies, regardless of their talent.

Great leaders select and surround themselves with individuals who are diverse in both demographic traits and thought. They create allies and leverage the team's opinions and collective talent. Leaders like Arthur pay for their independence with little followership, less accomplishment, and potentially their health. Arthur experienced all these consequences.

CHAPTER 33

THE AMERICAN LOUIS PHILIPPE

Millard Fillmore, 1850-1853

MILLARD FILLMORE, OUR 13TH president, viewed slavery as a political rather than moral issue. His support of the Compromise of 1850 pushed the slave issue back to the states. This series of bills passed by Congress avoided war and included the Fugitive Slave provision, which required that states return fugitive slaves to their former owners, even if they had fled to a free state. To Fillmore's credit, getting any compromise around slavery at the time was a rare accomplishment.

Fillmore was previously a lawyer who went on to hold both state and federal representative positions for his home state of New York. He later became Comptroller of New York before being elected vice president on the Whig party ticket with Zachary Taylor in 1848. He came to the presidency following Taylor's sudden death in 1850 and served out the remaining three years of the term.

An early champion of commercial expansion in the Pacific, Fillmore's foreign policy was quite good. He opened trade with Japan and averted several potential international conflicts (Cuba, Hawaii, Eastern Europe, and Central America) that could have escalated into war.

Fillmore was one of a series of pre-Civil War presidents who failed to address our nation's root issue at the time. Ultimately, his legacy of supporting the Compromise of 1850 angered both the pro- and anti-slavery factions and brought down the Whig party. Fillmore was the last U.S.

president not to be affiliated with either the Democratic or Republican party.

Lessons in Leadership

Not addressing and dealing with the root of the problem is one of the common issues of failed leaders. Throughout my career, I witnessed countless examples of owners or leaders who did not properly invest in where the marketplace was heading because they didn't want to deal with the near-term pain the changes may have caused. I saw this most around investing in technology. Organizations would allow groups to operate independently rather than collectively. Instead of investing in client preferences, they protected their employees' desire for comfort and control. In these cases, the root problem was short-sightedness and fear of change.

The root issue is often a painful process to remedy. It may mean changing people, processes, policies, etc. It's usually very disruptive and costly. However, without addressing the root issue, a problem will continue to manifest itself as a future more significant problem with ultimately far greater costs. Like many presidents before and after him, Fillmore tried to deal with the symptom rather than the root problem.

An important leadership principle is to do small things well before they become big things. Most leaders don't get credit for avoiding a problem; it's typically taken for granted. On Fillmore's positive side is he averted larger problems with his proactive policies around international affairs.

Doing small things well to avoid a growing problem and taking the time to address root issues doesn't always gain popularity or even get one noticed. But one important rule of thumb to remember: If you want applause and approval all the time, don't become a leader.

CHAPTER 34

THE GREAT ENGINEER

Herbert Hoover, 1929-1933

OUR 31ST PRESIDENT WAS a successful businessman, engineer, and self-made millionaire. Prior to becoming president in 1929, Herbert Hoover also led the Commission for Relief in Belgium, an effort after World War I to feed Europe, served as Director of the U.S. Food and Drug Administration, and was the U.S. Secretary of Commerce under Presidents Harding and Coolidge.

During his time in office, Hoover increased the federal budget to provide more childcare and protection and achieved prison reform to include new facilities, federal training for guards, and dealing with overcrowding. He championed the St. Lawrence Seaway project and the construction of Hoover Dam. He also signed the Davis-Bacon Act, which required fair wages, benefits, and overtime for workers on government-funded construction projects.

For all his positive accomplishments though, Hoover will be forever remembered for presiding over the stock market crash of 1929 and the Great Depression that followed. The depression devastated the United States' economy. Unemployment rose to 25 percent, housing prices plummeted 67 percent, international trade collapsed by 65 percent, and deflation soared to around 10 percent.[4]

---

4 Sundar, Aakash. "History of Capital Markets, Part 2 - Great Depression through Dot-Com Bubble." FundingFuel, December 2, 2021. https://fundingfuel.com/2021/12/01/

Although known in his civilian life as a great humanitarian, Hoover was a terrible communicator and showed little empathy for the suffering caused by the Depression. He was the consummate technocrat who tried to run the presidency uncompromisingly. When the American people needed help, he gave them new rules.

The pain of economic collapse and the Great Depression left a lasting stain on Hoover's reputation and legacy. In the 1932 presidential election, Hoover soundly lost to Franklin D. Roosevelt and his promise of a "New Deal."

Hoover is an example of an individual who failed in one role but clearly succeeded in another. After World War II, President Harry Truman called upon Hoover to lead the European reconstruction and relief effort.

Lessons in Leadership

Leaders need to truly understand the needs of those they serve. Leading with poor communication and little empathy is a disaster waiting to happen. I have often shared with leaders the importance of understanding how and when to "pour it on" and when to "back it off." While rules and policies are critical, so is understanding their purpose. Too often, no one understands why rules and policies were put into place or when. A great leader will look at rules that negatively impact the people they serve to see if they can loosen the burden.

Another important leadership lesson is "right people, right places." Frequently people are placed into roles they shouldn't be in and not into roles where they could have a much greater impact. Some of that occurs because organizations "pigeonhole" talent and don't fully demonstrate an ability to diversify a leader's experiences. Great leaders invest in their people by giving them many experiences and placing them in roles that best utilize their skills and best serve the organization.

---

history-of-capital-markets-part-2-great-depression-through-dot-com-bubble/#:~:text=A%20 third%20of%20all%20banks,to%20help%20our%20floundering%20economy.

Hoover was probably the wrong person at the wrong time; something that organizations typically observe in retrospect. He was talented as an organizer, engineer, and businessperson. He could have served our country well while simply holding roles in government aligned with those skills and not the top spot. A reminder for many organizations.

CHAPTER 35

TRICKY DICK

Richard Nixon, 1969-1974

RICHARD NIXON, THE 37TH president of the United States, was the first and only president who resigned from office. Despite several positive domestic and international policies and actions, Nixon's legacy will always be marred by the stains of cover up, lying, and arrogance.

Nixon was a lawyer and tough politician who rose to national prominence with his aggressive examination of Alger Hiss, a government official and spy who allegedly gave secrets to the Russians. While serving in the U.S. House of Representatives, Nixon established himself as a strong anti-Communist, positioning his rise to the Senate, the Vice Presidency, and ultimately the White House.

To his credit, Nixon tackled some very important welfare reform policies, law enforcement issues, environmental projects, and civil rights initiatives. Even as a right-wing Republican, Nixon proposed a family-assistance program that would have provided a guaranteed income for the poor. He also was a champion of capitalized Supplemental Security Income (SSI), which provided guaranteed incomes for the elderly, blind, and disabled, and an automatic cost of living adjustment for Social Security recipients.

Nixon's efforts around civil rights are also worth noting. He created a "set aside" program to reserve a certain percentage of jobs on federal construction projects for minorities. He significantly reduced segregation in schools and created the Equal Employment Opportunity Commission (EEOC) during his term.

Domestically, Nixon's administration faced a challenging economic and inflationary period. His policies created high budget deficits and stagnant growth. International affairs were more the strong suit for the Nixon administration. He inherited the Vietnam war and, like his predecessor Lyndon Johnson, struggled to end the conflict. That was finally achieved when he signed the Paris Peace Accords in 1973.

Nixon's most significant achievement in foreign affairs centered around China, whose relationship with the U.S. had been estranged for more than twenty years. Nixon's outreach not only thawed U.S.-China relations but also helped to legitimize China as a world power. It also opened negotiations and created leverage with Russia. This led to the first in a series of Strategic Arms Limitations talks and treaties.

You cannot review Nixon's presidency without looking at his demise, though: Watergate. Nixon was a distrusting and suspicious person. Despite being well-positioned to win landslide reelection, Nixon's underlings broke into the Democratic Party's campaign office in the Watergate Hotel. It was a botched and poorly covered-up break-in. Eventually, through the work of the Washington Post and the power of the free press, the break-in was discovered, the cover up disclosed, and the "smoking gun" Watergate tapes discovered. Nixon was aware of and encouraged the cover up.

The Watergate scandal did more harm than just bringing down our 37th president. The investigation revealed that not only Nixon but also John Kennedy and Lyndon Johnson had grave hesitations about the Vietnam War that were not consistent with what they were telling the American public.

Lessons in Leadership

You could probably write a book of leadership lessons studying Richard Nixon alone. On a positive note, his tenacity is inspiring. Nixon overcame significant odds to rise to the top, was very focused, and had a clear vision for how he would lead.

Good communication skills are essential to good leadership. That includes knowing your audience and surroundings. During the first televised presidential debate with John F. Kennedy, during Nixon's first run for the presidency in 1960, Nixon didn't understand how his presence could impact his image. He didn't present well on TV, and as a result, his brand was harmed for the election, which Kennedy won handedly.

Another component of good communication skills is being honest and straightforward in dealing with an issue. As a senator in 1952, Nixon admitted in a nationally televised speech that he accepted a dog as a gift. This was a brilliant example of "nipping" a potential issue before it got big! Too bad Nixon later forgot that being upfront and honest could help avoid disaster.

We are all human and will make mistakes. Admit them. If it means asking for forgiveness, sincerely ask for it. Not trying to cover up should be a standard rule for all leaders. Most leaders will stumble in their careers. It's how they recover that creates their legacy.

Leaders should always have a healthy dose of suspicion. Understanding motives and measuring risk is part of the critical thinking necessary for all successful leaders. This is especially the case if you are susceptible to flattery and prone to arrogance. These qualities can easily lead to making poor decisions to look good. A suspicion that leads to paranoia needs to be addressed and weeded out, though. Having honest, truth-telling people around you and listening to them is your best tool for that.

Nixon's cover-up of Watergate forever eroded the office of the presidency as America lost faith in the office itself. Maybe there's value in this, though. Blindly following a leader can be dangerous. It's essential to have a healthy dose of skepticism and realize that top officials are not only capable of abusing power; without guardrails, unchecked power is likely to corrupt. Watergate shed light on the importance of transparency. The wide array of media sources available today can contribute to the problem. It's on us as citizens to understand the difference between verifiable facts, misinformation, and disinformation. We are easily misled if we consume only what we want to believe.

CHAPTER 36

THE CAREFUL DUTCHMAN

Martin Van Buren, 1837-1841

WHEN MARTIN VAN BUREN was elected in 1836, he became the first president who was born a U.S. citizen. Our 8th president of the United States was quite accomplished and prepared for office. He was a lawyer, the first attorney general of New York, U.S. senator, governor of New York, secretary of state, and vice president under Andrew Jackson. Two key events and accomplishments marked his presidency: he served during the national financial panic of 1837, and he was instrumental in forming the Democratic party.

Early into his presidency, Van Buren was faced with a national financial panic. Part of this panic was a carryover from Andrew Jackson transferring federal funds from the Bank of the United States to state banks. Van Buren proposed transferring federal funds from state banks to an independent treasury. Congress passed the independent treasury bill in 1840, but only after a bitter struggle split the party and caused economic calamity. Ultimately this led him to lose the support of the Democratic party. Interestingly, while the issue significantly diminished Van Buren's popularity and ultimately cost him a second term as president, when reviewing his recommendation, economists today generally support his decision.

Van Buren's unpopularity also grew in part due to a long and costly Seminole Indian war in Florida and his failure to support the annexation of Texas. Texas would have come into the union as a slave state, and Van Buren wanted to avoid more conflicts dividing the country around slavery.

While Van Buren's legacy is more negative than positive, he did play an essential role in establishing our nation's current political system. Establishing the Democratic party solidified a two-party system that has been the dominant structure ever since. Some today might wonder whether that has proven to be a positive or negative thing.

Van Buren's rise to the presidency was primarily due to "hooking his wagon" to his popular predecessor, Andrew Jackson. This allegiance made him less inclined to go against Jackson's policies, which proved to be damaging both to our economy and to Van Buren personally.

Lessons in Leadership

Leadership requires courage, and courage manifests itself in many forms. It may mean a new vision that deviates from the past, confidence when others doubt, or a willingness to go against the grain. Because Van Buren was so beholden to his predecessor, Andrew Jackson, he was slow to course-correct during the early stages of the financial panic. Learning from a mentor, sponsor, or predecessor has genuine value. Feeling you are always obligated to do things the way they did can be dangerous, though. Being courageous requires that you continually grow and learn from others. It also means that you address the root problem even if your predecessor caused it.

Great leaders create, develop, and protect their brand. Van Buren sacrificed his own brand by trying to reflect someone else's—in this case, Andrew Jackson. We are each our own person, and no one does "you" better than you!

CHAPTER 37

THE DARK HORSE PRESIDENT

Rutherford B. Hayes, 1877-1881

RUTHERFORD B. HAYES BECAME our 19th president after a very close election where he lost the popular vote and gained some questionable electoral votes. He was a little-known candidate, even within the Republican party. This former lawyer, congressman, and governor of Ohio was ultimately put into office after the Compromise of 1877. This compromise ended military occupation of the south, gave Democrats positions in government, and put Hayes in the White House. Coming into office his primary focus was to reform civil service. This attempt not only failed but also angered his own party.

Hayes was caught up in immigration, specifically Chinese immigration in the west. The issue was a group of citizens who thought the Chinese immigrants were taking American jobs. Ultimately Hayes vetoed a bill restricting immigration of Chinese workers, but reductions were established.

Hayes is most remembered for being the president who ended Reconstruction, the Union's commitment to rebuilding the South after the civil war. In ending Reconstruction, the Republican party's commitment to equal rights for formerly enslaved people was also abandoned, setting up a century of segregation and discrimination. To be fair, Hayes alone didn't cause the problem. He did misjudge its potential long-term effect and stop any real progress. Until the 1960s, his successors did little to solve the issue either. Reconstruction, while effective as a theory, turned out to be flawed in reality. The South needed a much more comprehensive program, like the Marshall Plan, to rebuild and address civil rights issues.

To his credit, Hayes signed an act in 1879 permitting female lawyers to practice before the Supreme Court, forty years prior to women having the right to vote.

Hayes modeled his presidency on that of John Quincy Adams. Both were men of high integrity and character. Like Adams, he was a poor communicator, though, and never won the necessary support from Congress to achieve his goals. Knowing he didn't have a chance at reelection, Hayes did not seek a second term.

Lessons in Leadership

Leaders with a strong moral compass are concerned about who they serve. Hayes was a man of character with a strong sense of right and wrong who didn't translate his beliefs into action. He walked away from Reconstruction, which impacted civil rights, yet he focused his efforts on humanitarian causes after office. His view of what was right and wrong didn't include protecting or even considering all he served.

Hayes wasn't a great communicator. Great leaders are not only strong communicators, but they also use the skill to gain followership. Hayes' lack of communication hurt his ability to team with Congress and work together to get anything done well.

Finally, Hayes naively thought Reconstruction was a philosophy, not a comprehensive plan. He didn't spend time or energy on addressing the problematic issues at their core, diagnosing how deep they really went, or creating a comprehensive plan to implement lasting and effective change that could have healed the south and better re-united the nation.

CHAPTER 38

OLD ROUGH AND READY

Zachary Taylor, 1849-1850

ZACHARY TAYLOR, OUR 12TH president, was a decorated major general in the Mexican-American War and a national hero. Taylor was not a politician. His military career made him a strong nationalist and he ran the presidential race as a Whig.

Politically, Taylor was a reluctant leader. While his goal in office was to preserve the Union, he showed a lack of passion for dealing with slavery, the primary issue of the day. He did nothing to address it. Taylor himself was a slave owner but kept his distance from the issue. Unfortunately, he also kept his distance from his cabinet and Congress.

Taylor's legacy as a strong military leader was washed aside by politics. During his short term in office, he opposed adding slave states and attempted to add California as a free state, but to no avail. His efforts did lead to the Compromise of 1850, which passed after his death.

Sadly, there are no notable accomplishments from Zachary Taylor's administration. He died of cholera just sixteen months into office.

Lessons in Leadership

Selecting someone who is popular yet looks good only on paper is a common error by organizations, political parties, and voters. Leaders need to be prepared and genuinely committed to the role. Although popular,

Zachary Taylor was ill-equipped to lead the country as president. It seemed his heart just wasn't in it.

Taylor didn't deal with slavery, the primary issue facing the country at the time. Like others who avoid root issues and try to "decorate" the effects, they only prolong the problem. I would rather see a leader create a well-thought-out strategy and fail than work around a problem or ignore that it exists. To be fair, slavery was sanctioned by both Congress and the Supreme Court at the time. Tackling this root issue would have been Herculean, but all significant change begins with the courage to identify the problem and start the process.

It's hard to face tough issues. We don't want to do the unpopular thing. We don't want to do the difficult, lonely work of doing the job right. At the end of the day Taylor, like many failed leaders, should not have taken on something he didn't have the passion for doing.

CHAPTER 39

Takeaways on the Bottom Twelve

AS I READ THE biographies of U.S. presidents, I often wondered, were the great ones notable because they rose during a particular crisis, or would they have been great in any period? I've concluded that it's a matter of opinion. I believe those with outstanding leadership attributes would have been successful and notable in any circumstance at any time. I've also concluded that other, less-great presidents were influenced by self-interest, fear, caution, or arrogance. They probably would have faced failure at some point under any circumstance. I'd like to think that most of us need to believe that bad behavior eventually gets its due.

The twelve presidents that constitute the bottom of my list of presidents as viewed through the lens of leadership were quite unlike the great ones. The great ones rose to the difficult circumstances they faced. They demonstrated incredible fortitude, courage, focus, and determination. They truly believed in their vision for the country and were willing to sacrifice their self-interest and popularity to achieve it. The common ground of these bottom presidents was that they failed to address the root issues of the problems. Their biggest concern was to stay in power, be popular, and lead without regard to being followed. Most served their selfish interests over the good of the country. History isn't kind to such leaders, in politics or business.

PART FOUR

The Big Middle

CHAPTER 40

Thoughts on "The Big Middle"

AS I THINK ABOUT my own life and career and who has influenced me, I realize I've learned the most from a collection of people who will never be recognized for their leadership, but who were—and are—great influencers. Rarely do we quote a third-grade teacher or refer to the actions of a service person when looking at "profiles in courage" from our own lives. But we all have an opportunity to have a lasting impact on people we encounter; not just in our workplaces, but everywhere we go, and every time we interact with others.

Between the "top" and "bottom" is a group of eighteen presidents who competently served our country. I want to pay tribute to these non-distinguishable but impactful leaders of our nation. I think it's important not to overlook this group, which I call "the big middle." Too often in life, we focus on only the "best" and "worst." Those in the middle are largely forgotten; yet what differentiates them may have been nothing more than the circumstances of the day. Many of these leaders made significant decisions that impacted our country and the world both positively and negatively.

While a single president may be forgettable, their contributions shouldn't be. As with my top twelve and bottom twelve presidents, my objective in writing about each of these middle leaders individually is to recognize their unique strengths and failures and point out leadership principles.

I will not rank these remaining eighteen middle presidents. Instead, for the reader's ease, I will review them in the chronological order they served, beginning with the earliest. This will give us the added benefit of comparing individuals in a particular period. As with the other presidents, it's easy to fall into the trap of reviewing this group looking through a 21st-century lens. I will do my best to avoid that pitfall. It's unfair to them and would alter my views on their accomplishments or failures, as well as the leadership lessons.

All of us, regardless of our role, have an opportunity to shape lives. How we act, treat others, and respond to difficulties can greatly influence an attitude, opinion, or even career. Leaders have so much responsibility. A bad teacher can have a lasting impact on a student and future adult. An empathetic person can significantly affect another person's attitude and behavior. Acts of kindness and respect have a ripple effect on individuals and societies, as do rudeness and disrespect.

Not everyone should be in a leadership role. Those who can't trust probably can't be trusted. Those who serve themselves and their cronies' interests first create reluctant followership at best. Those who abuse power and don't take responsibility for their decisions don't usually last.

For some of these middle presidents, their negative traits outweighed their accomplishments in office. Others served with great intentions and maybe didn't achieve their desired outcomes. Circumstances outside of their control derailed their plans. These situations also teach leadership lessons. A leader's impact—both good and bad—is not always immediately realized. Many leaders' values are revealed through the test of time.

The "big middle" of presidents each brought value to our country. Some were in office during relatively benign periods of history, so it was difficult for them to have made a truly lasting mark. Some failures were self-inflicted. Several within this group did a few things well but had one or two failures that damaged their legacy.

Historians have moved several in this group either up or down with time and historical perspective. While not recognized for their greatness or popularity, they, like many leaders we encounter in our daily lives, proved to be part of the larger picture. They added a piece, sharpened a part, or avoided a potentially fatal flaw. The unknowns, the quiet ones, and the unspectacular are sometimes those who best help make us, our country, and our companies a little better.

CHAPTER 41

THE COLOSSUS OF INDEPENDENCE

John Adams, 1797-1801

JOHN ADAMS, OUR NATION'S second president, played an important role in the American Revolution. He was a delegate to the First Continental Congress and served on a committee responsible for structuring the Declaration of Independence. Adams was also instrumental in negotiating the 1783 Treaty of Paris that ended the Revolutionary war.

Adams was a versatile leader. Educated as a lawyer, he served as a diplomat and was the United States' first ambassador to Britain and later first vice president. He was also a prominent political author.

Beyond the foundational work he did as a "founding father," one of Adams' most outstanding contributions to our country was the appointment of John Marshall as the Chief Justice of the Supreme Court. Marshall played a significant role in developing the American legal system and firmed up the independence of the American judiciary branch. This act positioned the balance of power that has stood the test of time and is arguably one of the biggest reasons why the United States' democracy has been an extraordinary success on the world stage.

For all his foundational work, John Adams' support of the Alien and Seditions Acts was a blemish on his legacy. This legislation was four collective laws that made it harder for an immigrant to become a citizen, criminalized making a false statement critical of the federal government, and allowed the president to imprison and deport those who did. Also,

Adams was known for profound political partisanship. While partisanship has unfortunately remained a challenge for our government's ability to operate effectively and efficiently, the fact that the earliest behaviors went unchecked indirectly led to the intractability of this generally accepted behavior today.

Adams had a reputation for being obnoxious, opinionated, argumentative, and unpopular, which presumably led him to be a one-term president.

To his credit, Adams had an incredible partner in his wife, Abigail. One of her most famous quotes in a letter she penned to him in 1776 when John was participating in the Continental Congress was to "remember the ladies." "Do not put such unlimited power into the hands of the husbands. Remember all men would be tyrants if they could," she wrote. While this didn't change women's rights (or lack thereof) at the time, it did speak to the immense value of a strong partner. Abigail Adams planted an important seed.

Lessons in Leadership

John Adams' greatest accomplishment is a true sign of outstanding leadership: the appointment of John Marshall. Who a leader attracts, hires, and develops into roles is not only key to their present success but one of the best ways to build a legacy. Too many presidents surrounded themselves with cronies and average talent. When you attract and promote the best, you have given the organization—or in this case, the country—a lasting gift.

No matter how talented, experienced, or educated you are, if you are known to cause dissension, seen as obnoxious, and generally not liked, you won't last long in a leadership role. Arrogance is toxic and needs to be held in check. It tends to creep up slowly and if not managed it overruns not only your work but also your daily life. You may think it makes you a strong leader, board member, advocate, parent, friend, or neighbor, but honestly, if that's what you are known for, you won't be remembered as "great."

CHAPTER 42

FATHER OF THE CONSTITUTION

James Madison, 1809-1817

JAMES MADISON, ALONG WITH fellow writers of the Federalist Papers, Alexander Hamilton and John Jay, convinced his fellow delegates to form a federal government with checks and balances. Madison's Federalist Paper #10, which advocated for representative democracy, is among the most highly regarded of all political writings.

Our 4th president of the United States was not only a founding father but is also considered to be the father of the Constitution. His scholarly research and skillful writing effectively moved the thirteen original colonies to completely change the original Articles of Confederation into a new Constitution. This was critically important, as it shifted a strong state power and weak central government to a strong national government with strong state representatives. This was known as "The Virginia Plan."

Madison was also credited with drafting the Bill of Rights. This assurance of personal freedoms and rights both tipped the scales to ratify our Constitution and became the lasting backbone of our country's government.

Madison was a skilled diplomat, gifted statesman, and served as secretary of state under Thomas Jefferson. He also formed the second Bank of the United States and assisted Jefferson in securing the Louisiana Territory purchase.

Madison's wife and First Lady, Dolly, was a great benefit to our country. Dolly established many precedents that her successors would follow, including working with charities and various organizations on social issues. She also oversaw the decoration of the executive mansion to reflect the importance of the presidency.

Madison's biggest failure as president was succumbing to the pressure of his opponents in Congress to declare war on Britain, later known as the War of 1812. This conflict between America and its indigenous allies on one side and the British and their indigenous allies on the other allowed the new country to fall into a useless and wasteful war during a very vulnerable period of our history.

British forces burned the U.S. Capitol and the White House under Madison's watch. He allegedly fled Washington, D.C. before the British invaded, fearing being captured. His wife Dolly was left behind—at his direction—to save valuables, including a portrait of George Washington. There are conflicting stories about why she was in the White House while he was gone. Regardless of why, it's not something you would expect from a great leader, not to mention a great husband!

Lessons in Leadership

Great leaders do their homework. They study the works of others to know the strengths and weaknesses of a strategy before executing their plans. James Madison was an avid learner and did his research. The masterpiece of the Constitution of the United States is a compilation of the Magna Carta, Roman Law, and the influential thinking of a 17th century Englishman, John Locke.

Great leaders focus on a few items that make a difference when done well. Madison exemplified that behavior. He used his wisdom and communication skills to move the delegates of the Constitutional Convention, who intended only to amend the articles of confederation, into creating a new Constitution.

Unfortunately, Madison lacked the courage to address the underlying issue of a trade embargo placed by his predecessor, Jefferson, and outside pressure forced him into the error of declaring war on Britain. Great leaders measure risk when making major decisions. Losing popularity is far better than losing your country. Madison nearly did just that with the War of 1812.

One of Madison's strengths was that he chose a strong life partner. Great leaders can't do it on their own. They surround themselves with wise counsel and emotional support, which often comes from home. I, for one, can say much of my success in life can be attributed to a strong, loving, affirming, and supportive spouse.

CHAPTER 43

OLD MAN ELOQUENT

John Quincy Adams, 1825-1829

JOHN QUINCY ADAMS WAS our nation's 6th president and the first of two father/son presidents. Adams was a one-term president, and the contributions he made to the United States before he was president (and after) were far more significant than the ones he made while in the executive office. In 1785, he was assigned as the first U.S. Minister to Great Britain. His skills in foreign affairs later served all five of the presidents who preceded him. For example, in 1794, George Washington appointed him as Ambassador to The Netherlands, a significant financial power of the day. His father, President John Adams, appointed him as the U.S. Minister Resident to Prussia. Adams was the chief negotiator for the U.S. in the Treaty of Ghent, the agreement that ended the War of 1812. He is considered by many scholars to have been one of America's greatest secretaries of state. He resolved complicated and long-standing boundary issues and improved relations with Britain and Canada, with whom the disputes occurred. He was the author of the foreign policy that opposed European colonialism in North America, later enacted as the Monroe Doctrine.

John Q. Adams also served in the U.S. House of Representatives for seventeen years after leaving office. He died on the House floor after suffering a severe stroke. He literally gave his life to serving this country.

So why did he fail to get re-elected? Why was he not seen as successful? To understand this, one needs to look at how he came into office.

Adams lost the popular vote and had fewer electoral votes than Andrew Jackson in 1824. In what was called the "Corrupt Bargain," Adams got support from the fourth leading candidate, Henry Clay, by making him secretary of state when the election went to the House for vote. Andrew Jackson, who also ran, had won the popular vote. Adams could never shake the "House" bargain or his father's poor reputation and was seen as guilty by association.

Lessons in Leadership

Just because you're good at certain jobs doesn't mean you should be moved to the top position. When leaders are selected, they are typically chosen for their past results rather than current and future skills needed for the role. The tendency to pre-select instead of evaluating what future skills are most needed causes organizations and countries to pick the wrong person to lead. Adams was very pragmatic and had a strict moral view of life. It served him well in negotiating property lines, but his uncompromising and somewhat condescending approach didn't serve him well as president. As a result, very little of his progressive and important infrastructure plans for the growing county succeeded.

One of the most essential roles in leadership development and growth is mentorship. Mentorship should not be forced and should last only as long as both parties feel there is value. The mentor and mentee need to realize when that relationship may need new insights. To only go through the motions is counterproductive.

Whom you "hook your wagon to" is so important. I've seen many average leaders rise to the top with the right connections. I've also seen some of the very best talent get either pushed aside or have careers stalled because of whom they were aligned with.

Great leaders understand that how we communicate can be as important as what we communicate. Adams demonstrates leadership lessons on compromise and communications. He was intelligent and had a strong grasp of issues. However, he alienated others by being unwilling to compromise and speaking condescendingly. Despite some impressive work, it ultimately cost him an election and a legacy buried in U.S. history books.

I remind leaders to "not die on every hill." Part of this is about compromise. Part of it is about perception. Most of us have difficulty following or respecting someone who must always be right. Everyone agrees with that until they realize they have become that person!

CHAPTER 44

OLD HICKORY

Andrew Jackson, 1829-1837

ANDREW JACKSON WAS KNOWN as "the people's president." Our nation's 7th president was plain-spoken and seen as the first president who stood for the common person. Before being elected to the presidency, Jackson was a lawyer, a general in the United States Army, and served in both the House of Representatives and Senate. His military mindset and strong passion for preserving the country were the foundation of his presidency.

Motivated by a strong desire for control, Jackson was the first president who began to shift policymaking from Congress to the Executive Office using veto power. He also used his popularity to push for stronger federal laws, moving the country away from state-first agendas that had been driving the country's growth to this point.

Jackson was known as an expansionist. His "Jacksonian democracy" became the nation's dominant political view and the foundation of today's Democratic party. During this era, voting rights were expanded to include the commoner as opposed to only land-owning white men. While that may be difficult to understand as an accomplishment, from the early to mid-1800s, restrictions in voting were common throughout democratic governments around the world. Norway, Germany, and France all had income level requirements and reserved voting rights for men only.[5]

Jackson used tariffs to improve trade. He also took on the corruption that had infiltrated Washington, D.C., starting with revoking the charter of the Second Bank of the United States, which was theoretically a private corporation that served as a government-sponsored monopoly. Although breaking down a government-sponsored monopoly made a lot of sense, the bank was the backbone of our financial system, and the Centralized Treasury System had not yet been built to replace it.

His dealings with Native Americans, especially the enactment of policies that included ethnic cleansing and the removal of Indian tribes from their ancestral lands to make room for other settlers (The Trail of Tears), was a stain on Jackson's legacy. Another failure was his appointment of Roger Taney to the Supreme Court in 1835. Taney was later known for the Dred-Scott decision, which essentially declared that African Americans were non-citizens who could not vote or file a lawsuit.

Under Jackson's leadership, the country moved to be more aligned with the Constitution's foundational principle of " . . . by the people, for the people." While the steps were admittedly small, they did nudge the nation in the direction of full inclusivity for all people, a goal we are still working towards today as a society.

Lessons in Leadership

Great leaders understand the importance of gaining the hearts of the people they serve. There is power in leaders who can relate to those they serve and hear the voice of the unheard. Jackson's intentions were generally for the best for the common person. He cared for the flock and not the fleece and was broadly admired for this reputation. He developed not only strong

---

5 Zinkina, Julia, Oleg A Alekseenko, and Ilya V Ilyin. "Global Struggle for Suffrage Expansion: The European Case for Male Suffrage in the Nineteenth Century." Social Studies. Accessed May 31, 2022. https://www.sociostudies.org/almanac/articles/global_struggle/.

followership, but he also greatly influenced how the office operated from his time in office until FDR.

Jackson also demonstrated courage. He strongly opposed his vice president, John C. Calhoun, and Henry Clay, a senior senator—both fellow southerners—over state versus federal rights. State rights at the time were primarily to protect slavery, and Jackson stood firmly for the betterment of the country over regional alliances. Great leaders will stand on principles of the greater good over the interests and benefits of a few.

Jackson's shortcoming of failing to address what we now see as human rights violations was generally overlooked because the citizens of the day perceived his intentions as good. Unfortunately, the "flock" he cared for did not include marginalized populations. But understanding the leader's true intention is what they should be judged for. We all make mistakes. We all misjudge.

CHAPTER 45

TIPPECANOE

William Henry Harrison, 1841

WILLIAM HENRY HARRISON, OUR 9th president, served just thirty-one days in office. Partly to show his vitality, Harrison stood outside
on his cold and wet inauguration day and delivered the longest inaugural
address in U.S. history. After his two-hour speech and an outdoor three-
hour receiving line followed by three inaugural balls, Harrison fell ill, con-
tracted pneumonia, and died one month after taking office. Whether the
cold and rain caused his illness has been debated, but the fact remains that
he didn't live long after that fateful day.

Harrison was a decorated Army Captain, U.S. Congressman, the
Northwest Territory's first congressional delegate, and eventually governor of the Indiana Territory. As governor, he was given authority to negotiate treaties. Typical of most U.S. treaties with Native Americans, most
were one-sided and signed under duress. Harrison forged one treaty that
led to the Battle of Tippecanoe (named for the attack's location near the
Tippecanoe River in Indiana) against the great Shawnee Indian leader,
Tecumseh. Harrison not only led the Battle of Tippecanoe but also later
exploited the overblown victory to include a Whig party slogan during his
presidential campaign. "Tippecanoe" became his presidential nickname.

One of Harrison's most important accomplishments was after he "left"
office. Article 11, Section 1, Clause 6 of the United States Constitution was

insufficient and needed to be addressed.[6] This article spoke to presidential succession. It outlined that the vice president would take over duties and powers in the event of a president's death, removal, resignation, or inability. What was untested and unclear was, did the vice president formally become the president, or just assume the duties of office? Interestingly, following Harrison's death, his cabinet viewed John Tyler, the vice president, as vice president and acting president. Tyler had other ideas and saw that he had not only the power but also the position. The cabinet consulted the Chief Justice of the Supreme Court. After consultation, Tyler was sworn in as the 10th president of the United States. This precedent set in 1841 was followed seven times when an incumbent president died. It was finally formalized into the Constitution in 1967 as part of the 25th amendment.

Compounding this unusual transition was the fact that Harrison was a Whig candidate who, along with his appointed Whig cabinet, was set to execute a Whig agenda. Tyler had other ideas and not only abandoned the agenda, but also abandoned the party.

Lessons in Leadership

Understanding your audience and environment is an important leadership communication skill. Harrison overlooked this and gave the longest inaugural speech to date, a self-written speech that exceeded 8,400 words on a cold and wet day. The extended exposure to harsh weather conditions not only endangered him but also jeopardized all who had to stand through it. I certainly have never stood in the cold rain for two hours to hear a speech! But I have sat through countless speeches that were entirely too long and incoherent. Many leaders forget to understand that presentations need a point. They shouldn't use the platform for adoration or "winging it." That

---

6 Gillespie, Janine Turner and Cathy. "Article II, Section 1, Clause 6 of the United States Constitution." Constituting America. Janine Turner and Cathy Gillespie http://constitutingamerica.org/wp-content/uploads/2021/10/logo_web_white_280x62.png, March 14, 2020. https://constitutingamerica.org/april-21-2011-%E2%80%93-article-ii-section-1-clause-6-of-the-united-states-constitution-%E2%80%93-guest-essayist-joe-postell-university-of-colorado-at-colorado-springs/.

doesn't show their personal side, as many believe. It shows their incompetent side.

Leaders should have a core speech that outlines their own or their organization's priorities and goals. They should have a clear, concise message they can give in a short or long version, customized as appropriate for the demographics of their audience. I'm amazed at how awkward some leaders can be when presenting basic messages. The great ones practice. They learn from their mistakes. They understand their audience and surroundings, and they inspire.

Another leadership lesson demonstrated by Harrison's brief presidency is talent placement. His running mate, John Tyler, was not aligned with Harrison's agenda and priorities. Leaders must do their homework to ensure succession planning has the right people in place when the unforeseen becomes reality.

CHAPTER 46

UNCLE SAM GRANT

Ulysses S. Grant, 1869-1877

ULYSSES S. GRANT, OUR 18th president, is an example of extremes. He was a strong leader in chaos who was known to escape into heavy drinking in quiet times. Grant was self-made. He rose from the bottom rung of society as a poor farmer, failed businessman, and outcast soldier to become the leader of the Union Army and eventual president of the United States. Grant ran as a Republican and won two presidential terms.

Grant was far less accomplished than his Union Army predecessors. Although a West Point graduate, he was not a gifted student like his Confederate Army peers. Even his closest ally, General William T. Sherman, questioned his knowledge and ability to lead a war effort. But as it turned out, Grant proved to be a very accomplished battlefield leader. And on the long path to reunification, his "peaceful reconstruction" began with allowing Confederate General Robert E. Lee's troops to be fed and provided for immediately following Lee's surrender. This was a monumental first step in rebuilding the broken Union.

Grant served as president during the Reconstruction Era, a period marked by the southern states' need to change from a slavery-based economy and be brought back into the Union against their will. Grant, unlike his predecessors, had a vision that the federal government was there to enforce the civil rights of all. Under his leadership, Congress passed the fifteenth amendment, which gave African Americans the right to vote. Grant took this amendment one step further through the first Enforcement Act of 1871, which permitted federal oversight at polls to ensure voting rights. He called on former Confederate leaders, including his friend from the Confederate Army, James Longstreet, to help enforce these laws.

The Department of Justice was formed under Grant's leadership, as was the Office of the Solicitor General, a position that represented the U.S. government before the Supreme Court. He signed legislation establishing Yellowstone National Park, our nation's first national park. He also passed the influential Treaty of Washington, which permanently established peace and a strong relationship with Canada and Great Britain.

Grant's strength of believing in his people and his weakness of using only his instincts gave him major blind spots though. An example of how this hurt his presidency was his selection of former Union general Orville Babcock as his personal assistant. Babcock was part of the "Whiskey Ring," which defrauded the government of millions of dollars in taxes on whiskey. Grant defended him.

While Grant's administration was marked with corruption, his character was best evidenced by his reflection and acknowledgment of his failings: "My failures have been errors of judgment, not of intent." I wonder how many leaders would readily admit their flaws, publicly and unsolicited.

Lessons in Leadership

Grant's ability to be courageous and calm during a crisis is a model for leaders. Those who followed him would say he could "slow his mind to gain clarity." Grant also showed empathy for those he led, and those he opposed. In fact, two of the Confederate generals he fought were pallbearers at his funeral.

Leaders need balance in life and need to take care of themselves. Grant didn't. He was a heavy cigar smoker, which presumably later led to his death from throat cancer. He used alcohol as a crutch. Excessive drinking became his brand and never left him. Brands are so important and, once set, difficult to alter.

We are all human, and all have flaws. Grant was partly a product of an era that did not understand alcoholism as a disease rather than a weakness.

Many leaders don't inspect what they expect. Words and promises over sustainable actions easily fool them. Grant trusted without inspection. This continued to plague him throughout his life, affecting him both personally and financially. He blindly trusted his friends, placing them in key roles in his cabinet over more qualified people. Many leaders surround themselves with people they know and like to hang out with. It's admirable to care and trust, just not blindly.

Grant possessed a considerable measure of common sense, an unshakeable faith in victory, and an ability to gain a sense of calm and clarity during the most challenging times. Think about that for a second, relative to any leader you've known: common sense, incredible belief in the people you lead, a relentless belief in success, and a calm, clear mind during the most chaotic times. I'm not sure you can teach these characteristics. You may be able to reinforce them, but very few leaders use previous disasters to become teaching moments for future leaders.

Great leaders are learners. Grant learned from his mistakes and brushed off failures as part of the process. He was undoubtedly a complex and enigmatic leader.

CHAPTER 47

PREACHER JIM

James Garfield, 1881

JAMES GARFIELD WAS ONE of eight U.S. presidents who died in office and four killed by an assassin's bullet. Sadly, he probably didn't need to die. His death was later determined to be caused not by the bullet but rather by a surgeon's unsterilized scalpel. This medical negligence led to blood poisoning, Garfield's actual cause of death.

Garfield, our nation's 20th president, was born into poverty in Ohio. He served as a major general in the Union Army, in the Ohio Senate, and later the U.S. House of Representatives. He was chosen as his party's "dark horse" candidate and won the presidency in 1880. He served from March to September of 1881, the second shortest term of any president.

Despite his presidency lasting only a few months, Garfield left his mark on the office and our country. His first significant accomplishment was not caving to appointing Senate picks for cabinet positions. This stand against the patronage system set an important precedent. Garfield was also very financially astute and worked with Treasury Secretary William Windom to refinance our government bond portfolio so that it saved the United States five percent of the U.S. GDP. He cleaned up corruption in the U.S. Postal System and pushed hard for the economic rights of African Americans. Garfield also made a key Supreme Court appointment and proposed the Pendleton Civil Service Reform Act, which required federal government jobs to be awarded based on merit. This legislation was later signed by his successor, Chester Arthur.

Within a short time, Garfield supported civil rights, curbed incestuous cronyism that plagued many previous administrations, changed the government hiring process to merit-based, supported Chinese immigration, and saved the U.S. significant expense with bond restructure. All in all, rather impressive for just six months in office!

I would imagine and believe many historians would agree that had James Garfield not been shot by a disgruntled job seeker, he would have been one of our more popular presidents. Unfortunately, we will never know.

Lessons in Leadership

Great leaders don't make hiring decisions based on who or what is popular; they make hiring decisions based on merit. James Garfield bucked political insider influence and made appointments to his cabinet based on who was best for the job.

Garfield demonstrated having a strong vision and he created strategies to execute this vision. As a result, he was able to address multiple issues quickly. Many leaders find it challenging to focus on the tough areas first. Garfield didn't avoid the challenge and addressed the difficult problems head-on. Great leaders make this their priority.

Garfield not only stressed fiscal responsibility but was directly engaged in the activities that created significant savings for the country. Great leaders measure what's important and hold themselves and others to outcomes. If it's important, measure it!

Like many leaders, Garfield was someone who was appreciated for how good he was at his job after his death. One of the best testaments to a leader is when successors speak highly of what they accomplished, even if they have a different agenda.

CHAPTER 48

UNCLE JUMBO

Grover Cleveland, 1885-1889, 1893-1897

GROVER CLEVELAND WAS OUR 22nd and 24th president of the United States and the only president to serve two non-consecutive terms. Prior to his presidencies, he was the mayor of Buffalo, New York, and later governor of the state. After winning the general election in 1884, Cleveland was defeated by Benjamin Harrison in 1888. Harrison supported tariffs backed by industrialists and factory workers, while Cleveland saw the tariffs as unfair to consumers. Cleveland had also alienated many veterans and farmers with his opposition to civil war pensions. But Cleveland came back to defeat Harrison in 1892, primarily because Harrison had failed to gain Congressional support for his initiatives. His personality was seen as stiff and distant, enough to tip the scales back to his predecessor.

Cleveland was a conservative Democrat and crusader for both fiscal conservatism and political reform. Committed to the principles of classical liberalism, he supported free markets, civil liberties, and economic and political freedoms. As a result, he was able to draw support for his agenda from conservative Republicans as well as his own Democratic party. Cleveland's bipartisan appeal allowed him to be one of just two Democrats elected to the White House between 1861 and 1933, Woodrow Wilson being the other.

Cleveland was a principled man who wasn't afraid to attack corruption and powerful business interests. In 1887 he signed the Interstate

Commerce Act, which regulated the powerful railroad industry and demanded the return of a significant amount of land the railroads had "acquired." He also focused on strengthening our military, with a particular emphasis on rebuilding our coastal fortification systems. The nation's Naval fleet and Navy operations were modernized under his leadership.

The biggest failure came during Cleveland's second term in office with the Panic of 1893. This panic resulted in widespread unemployment and bank failures. While primarily the result of his predecessor Benjamin Harrison's actions, Cleveland's only response to this event was supporting a repeal of the Silver Purchase Act, which increased the amount of silver the government was required to purchase, intentionally creating inflation and a cheaper dollar.

This repeal did little to change the economic depression the panic had created. So, while his policies were perceived as honest and firm, they led to unrest among the American workforce and splintered the Democratic party.

Lessons in Leadership:

Making decisions that split from allies is not only difficult but rare. Cleveland wasn't intimidated by powerful forces. In his case, the major industry was railroads. Not only did he do the right thing by standing up to this powerful industry, but he also created long-term accountability for its actions.

Leaders are often more concerned about keeping support and staying elected than fixing the problems or doing the right thing, especially in politics. Any leader brave enough to stand firm in the face of criticism or rejection is on the path to respect and becoming what a true leader is called to be.

It's easy to focus on the "what" and lose sight of the "how." How one addresses problems, challenges, and criticisms is essential. The "what" for Cleveland was the Panic of 1893. He believed the Silver Purchase was the root of the problem. The "how" was his defensive reaction of repeal rather than working with Congress to address the overall economic weaknesses. Great leaders are not short-sighted and reactive. They think "big picture" and look for lasting solutions.

CHAPTER 49
THE HUMAN ICEBERG
Benjamin Harrison, 1889-1893

BENJAMIN HARRISON, OUR 23RD president of the United States, was the grandson of William Henry Harrison, our 9th president, and great-grandson of Benjamin Harrison V, who signed the Declaration of Independence. That's some serious leadership blood! A prominent lawyer and former senator from Indiana, Harrison was elected to the presidency in 1888. He was an outstanding public speaker but known to be quite awkward in small groups. He was a man of strong conviction with subjects he believed in.

As president, much of Harrison's agenda moved the U.S. toward being an empire-building nation. He supported annexing Hawaii and pushed for a trans-isthmus canal in Central America that later resulted in the building of the Panama Canal. Many historians feel his framework set the agenda for America's foreign policy for the next quarter-century.

Harrison supported the McKinley Tariff, which imposed historic protective trade rates. He also supported the Sherman Silver Purchase Act, by which the Treasury bought silver to create inflation, resulting in economic collapse shortly after he left office in 1893. This poorly managed domestic monetary policy caused financial ruin for many in the late 19th and early 20th centuries and likely cost Harrison a second term. More so than domestic policy oversights, Harrison's personality and style probably tarnished his record. He gave the impression that he didn't care.

The United States grew under Harrison's leadership. His administration brought six Western states into the Union, the largest number for any president: North Dakota, South Dakota, Montana, Washington, Idaho, and Wyoming.

Overall, Harrison's priorities were more focused on personal convictions than the country's needs. As a Restoration Era president, Harrison attempted legislation to improve civil rights for African Americans, but to no avail. Congressional support was simply not there.

Lessons in Leadership

Too many leaders support issues that only make them look good or are popular. While we greatly admire courage, it rarely gets rewarded as much as popularity. That's very unfortunate. Harrison was a man of strong moral character who stood on principle, even when it wasn't for his political gain and, in some cases, hurt his support.

Harrison was a great example of a leader who cared for those he served even though his communication style didn't reflect that. Known to be a man of character, Harrison was also stiff, formal, and disliked small talk. His awkwardness in social situations was probably a reflection of shyness as opposed to not caring though. But one doesn't need to be an extrovert to garner followership, which every leader must earn. Leaders who can't connect with those they lead struggle to gain support for their vision and strategies.

Leaders who have a lasting, positive effect on the people they serve focus on a few important issues that have the greatest impact or meet the most significant needs. Harrison focused primarily on international affairs, while his domestic policies floundered. We all have priorities. It's critical to have the best people assigned to each priority. At times that may not include you. Great leaders delegate, hold others accountable and own responsibility for outcomes.

CHAPTER 50

THE NAPOLEON OF PROTECTION

William McKinley, 1897-1901

WILLIAM MCKINLEY WAS THE last U.S. president to have served in the military during the Civil War. Our 25th president was previously a successful lawyer, U.S. Congressman, and two-term governor of Ohio. He was a reformer, an arbitrator during workers' strikes, and a protectionist president. He was elected for two terms and, unfortunately, was assassinated six months into his second term.

The primary focus of McKinley's early presidency was domestic policy, specifically economic expansion. Coming off the panic of 1893, which led to a Depression, McKinley used protectionism and tariffs—specifically the Dingley Act of 1897—to expand the economy. Tariffs are generally not seen as sustainable tools of economic expansion, however. McKinley's protectionism and heavy export tariffs would later negatively impact the United States.

McKinley restored the gold standard and expanded the influence of the executive office. He also opened trade with China and liberated Cuba by defeating the Spanish in the Spanish-American War in 1898. This one-hundred-day war also led to the U.S. acquisition of Puerto Rico, Guam, and the Philippine Islands.

McKinley leveraged the telephone as a means of communication and changed the approach on political campaign strategies to include utilizing the press and publicity to get his messages out. He also greatly expanded the presidential staff. The office of the President would never be the same.

Lessons in Leadership

Great leaders understand the importance of continually and consistently sharing their vision and strategies. McKinley was a good strategist who leveraged media and developing technology to promote his agenda. Known to "do his homework" before moving forward, he was self-assured and astute in decision-making.

Great leaders have courage and confidence. McKinley showed courage in standing on decisions that, although unpopular, he felt best served the country. While leaders need to be confident, the best remain humble. Overconfidence can lead to an inflated ego, a potential trap for failure.

Again, the importance of brand is worth considering with McKinley, who many perceived as a puppet to Marcus Hanna, an influential businessman and prominent senator from Ohio. Hanna was a political ally and the mastermind behind McKinley's campaigns. Although the relationship provided fodder for newspapers, McKinley certainly wasn't a "puppet." But once cast, a brand, whether negative or positive, is hard to change.

CHAPTER 51

BIG CHIEF

William Taft, 1909-1913

WILLIAM TAFT, OUR 27TH president, served one term as a Republican president. His presidency was sandwiched between the very popular and dynamic Theodore Roosevelt and the accomplished and strong Woodrow Wilson. As a result, he was somewhat of an overlooked president. He was always a judge at heart.

Before his presidency, Taft served the Ohio Superior Court and the Sixth Circuit Court of Appeals. He served as secretary of war in the Teddy Roosevelt administration. He was also named the first civilian governor of the Philippines and was seen as more an administrator than a politician.

Taft was not a pretentious man. He wasn't competitive and was a reluctant leader who was more comfortable on the judicial bench than behind a presidential desk. As a result, he was easily outmaneuvered by experienced politicians. Despite his relatively quiet presidency, he did work to protect against anti-trust busting, a significant accomplishment due to the proliferation of monopolies in that era. Taft pushed for tariff reform, including signing the Payne-Aldrich Act, a bill to raise tariffs on certain goods coming into the U.S. He was instrumental in establishing senatorial elections over state legislative appointments. He also empowered the Interstate Commerce Commission, which set railroad rates and mandated constitutional amendments regulating federal income tax.

Taft's greatest accomplishment was after leaving office, becoming the first and only former president to be appointed to the Supreme Court. He ultimately became the Chief Justice of the Supreme Court, thus holding the highest office in two of the three branches of government. This speaks to his multiple talents and contributions to the nation.

Taft's failures were probably more a result of his style, not judgment. The office had gained considerable power after President Teddy Roosevelt, and Taft relinquished that power. His somewhat conservative nature caused him to become narrowly focused and unable to mobilize others to get things accomplished.

Lessons in Leadership

Not all leaders are suited for their role yet might be outstanding in another position. Some are not cut out to lead people effectively at all. Leadership is a combination of attributes, talents, and characteristics that enable people to create a vision, set direction, and garner followership. Some people think they want to lead but don't have the competencies or passion to do so. A leadership role is not always the "next" logical step in a career. Taft didn't appear to have a heart for the presidency.

Leaders who are sandwiched between strong leaders can be viewed as weak—often much weaker than they are. Taft failed to leverage the momentum that had been established with the executive office, a common flaw of new leaders. He surrounded himself with only a few like-minded people, which stalled growth and innovation. Whom you surround yourself with is critical to success. Successful leaders balance their strengths and weaknesses with a strong supporting cast.

CHAPTER 52

SILENT CAL

Calvin Coolidge, 1923-1929

CALVIN COOLIDGE, OUR 30TH president, came to the role after President Warren Harding died in office. Coolidge was previously a lawyer from Massachusetts who became involved in state politics, eventually becoming governor. His response to the Boston Police Strike of 1919 placed him in the national spotlight as a man who could get things done. Two years later, he became Harding's vice president, a position he held for two years prior to taking over as president. Coolidge was reserved and, as his nickname "Silent Cal" suggests, a man of few words. His quiet manner, however, wasn't an indication of meekness but rather respect for the fact that as president, what you say matters.

Coolidge's accomplishments included cleaning up the corruption of the Harding administration (e.g., Teapot Dome). He led America through the economic recovery that followed World War I and the "Roaring Twenties" expansion. Coolidge was an advocate for smaller government and laissez-faire economic policy. He was a fiscal conservative focused on cutting taxes and letting business cycles expand unabated. He firmly believed that local problems were best solved locally and, even during a farm crisis, was slow to make federal government the solution.

While conservative, Coolidge was unique in that he was quite progressive around social issues. He stood against lynching and wouldn't allow members of the KKK to hold federal office. In 1924 he granted citizenship to all Native Americans, giving them far more rights than previous treaties and land ownership had. Despite his strong social leanings, he did have blind spots like immigration controls based on race and countries of origin.

As for foreign policy, Coolidge did not forgive European debt or lower import taxes that hurt European recovery following World War I. He did, however, support the Dawes Plan, which gave American private citizens the ability to purchase the debt of German loans.

Coolidge was a popular president and seen as a man of his word. In 1927, with a balanced federal budget and an expanding economy to his credit, he decided not to run for a second term even though he would likely have been reelected. His philosophy was that no president should be in office for more than two terms, even though he technically served just one- and one-half terms.

History has a mixed view of Coolidge. Not because of what he did in office, which was apparent, but what happened after he left. He was later criticized for how slowly he handled the farm crisis, caused by major flooding and loss, and his "small government" oversight approach, which led to the market crash in 1929. This crash led to the Great Depression.

Lessons in Leadership

Leaders with vision are constantly building for the future. Proactively identifying problems before they become major ones is a skill. Anything that is growing at an exorbitant pace isn't typically sustainable. Instead of relying on hope, one should always examine downside risk and controls. It's important to establish guardrails rather than clean up the aftermath. Coolidge should have used the time of rapid economic expansion to safeguard and protect against irrational exuberance. But that wasn't his style or policy.

Coolidge was slow to deal with the farm crisis. While I don't believe his approach was based on the political winds of the time but rather his core belief in a small federal government, he only reacted after witnessing the devastation. A leader should always do the right thing, regardless of the political climate, timing, and cost. Leadership is about courage, flexibility, owning up to, and fixing issues.

Great leaders take their tasks seriously but don't take themselves too seriously. Coolidge focused on identifying high-impact tasks and doing them well. Yet, in his "man of few words" style, he used humor and wit to reinforce messages. Sounds like my kind of guy!

CHAPTER 53

MR. NICE GUY

Gerald R. Ford, 1974-1977

GERALD FORD WAS NEVER elected as president or vice president. He stepped into both offices because of the disgrace of others. Prior to occupying the White House, Ford was a lawyer, lieutenant commander in the Navy, Michigan congressman, U.S. congressman, and speaker of the house. Under the terms of the 25th amendment, he became vice president after his predecessor Spiro Agnew resigned, and later became 38th president of the United States with Nixon's resignation on August 9, 1974. The country's trust for the White House was at an all-time low. Ford was known as a moderate, friendly, and honest politician. It would seem he was just what the nation needed at the time.

Upon entering the office, Ford faced an economy struggling with high inflation, stubborn unemployment, and general unrest following the Vietnam war. A Republican who wasn't conservative enough to appease the right-wing of his party or strong enough to convince the majority Democrats to adapt to his agenda, he struggled to advance his policies.

Ford made a few decisions early in his presidency that plagued his popularity. He announced a conditional amnesty program for those who evaded the draft or deserted during the Vietnam war. He chose Nelson Rockefeller, an established eastern liberal as vice president, fully alienating his party. And finally, in an effort to move the country forward, he pardoned Richard Nixon.

Politicians, legal scholars, and much of the press and public were critical of Ford's decision to pardon Nixon. There were rumors that Nixon agreed to resign only if Ford would pardon him. This proved to be unfounded and untrue. According to his attorney, Benton Becker, Ford's decision to pardon Nixon was based on a 1915 Supreme Court ruling, Burdick vs. the United States. The court ruled that a pardon carried an "imputation of guilt" and accepting a pardon was "an admission of guilt."[7]

Years later, Bob Woodward of the Washington Post, who broke the Watergate story and was very opposed to the pardon, said it was "an act of courage." Senator Ted Kennedy, a Democrat and early critic, later agreed that Ford made the right decision to move the country forward. The most compelling position came from Ben Veniste, a former Watergate prosecutor and Democrat. Veniste wrote in 2006 after Ford's death, " . . . The decision to pardon Nixon was a political judgment properly within the bounds of Ford's constitutional authority." He went further in this commentary for the Washington Post, saying "Gerry Ford acted in accord with what he sincerely felt were the best interests of the country."[8]

As with many issues, time heals and provides clarity. A Gallup poll taken shortly after the pardon showed that 53 percent of Americans disapproved of the decision. A little over a decade later, the sentiment changed to 39 percent disapproval.[9] While Americans today may either not remember or fail to have an opinion on the pardon, most would probably agree that this decision was the right thing to do for our country at the time.

Ford was a president that ended a recession, decreased inflation, reduced unemployment, improved farm incomes to record highs, navigated an energy crisis, and signed the Helsinki Accords that lessened tension with the Soviet Union, and yet was not reelected. It seemed the

---

7 Burdick v. United States, 236 U.S. 79, 89-90

8 "The Nixon Pardon in Constitutional Retrospect." National Constitution Center – constitutioncenter.org. https://constitutioncenter.org/blog/the-nixon-pardon-in-retrospect.

9 Carroll, Joseph. "Americans Grew to Accept Nixon's Pardon." Gallup.com. Gallup, April 11, 2021. https://news.gallup.com/poll/3157/americans-grew-accept-nixons-pardon.aspx.

country simply wanted to move on from the Nixon administration and everything associated.

Although he never got a chance to serve beyond the one-term, fill-in role, Ford moved the country forward. His legacy will remain as that of a reconciler and healer.

Lessons in Leadership

Leadership requires courage. Gerald Ford showed unwavering courage in deciding to pardon Richard Nixon. He knew popular opinion was not in his favor yet put the country's best interest over self-interest.

In May 2001, Ford received the John F. Kennedy Profile in Courage award. In accepting this award, he remarked: "The ultimate test of leadership is not the polls you take, but the risks you take. In the short run some risks prove overwhelming. Political courage can be self-defeating. But the greatest defeat of all would be to live without courage, for that would hardly be living at all."

Ford is an outstanding example of a strong brand. Throughout the writings on his life and presidency, there are common reflections from multiple authors, friends, and foes. Gerald Ford was an honest man, a likable man, and a thoughtful man. What an incredible legacy. Every leader should hope to be remembered for any of these qualities.

CHAPTER 54

JIMMY

Jimmy Carter, 1977-1981

JIMMY CARTER, OUR 39TH U.S. president, was known for being an outsider to the Washington political scene. This was seen as one of his strong suits in the election of 1976, after the Nixon/Ford era. Before becoming president, Jimmy was a graduate of the U.S. Naval Academy, peanut farmer, Georgia state senator, and governor of Georgia. Carter was an activist. He was an idealist. He came to Washington to make it more compassionate.

Carter loved process, and his administration ended up being more focused on process than quality outcomes. He came into the office facing domestic challenges of high inflation and high unemployment. While he was able to increase jobs and lower the budget deficit, high-interest rates and a stubbornly high inflation rate persisted. Its impact on the everyday American likely caused him to be a one-term president.

While in office, Carter did have several noteworthy accomplishments. He dealt with the energy crisis by establishing a national energy policy. He was instrumental in deregulating both the trucking and airline industries. He was a conservationist and expanded our national parks and protected millions of acres of the Alaskan wilderness. He created the Department of Education and increased social services. He was very deliberate in his push toward equal rights and appointed a record number of women and people of color to various government positions.

Internationally, Carter was known for the Camp David Accord, which secured an Israel/Egypt peace treaty and ultimately led to him winning the Nobel Peace Prize in 2002.

He also pushed for fair elections across the globe, normalized relations with China, and signed the SALT II Nuclear Limitations Treaty with the Soviet Union.

In addition to the economic challenges that negatively impacted Carter's presidency, he also had an embarrassing Iranian hostage crisis that was not fully resolved until after he left office.

Carter, somewhat like Hoover, is more known for his positive impact after his presidency than in the White House. His compassion continued to mark his post-presidency life, and he is known today as a first-class humanitarian. In addition to establishing the Carter Center to Advance Human Rights and Alleviate Human Suffering, Carter is a longtime avid supporter of Habitat for Humanity. He also continued efforts to ensure fair elections as an election observer in nearly forty countries. Carter ultimately earned a United Nations Human Rights prize in 1998, the Presidential Medal of Freedom in 1999, and the Nobel Peace Prize in 2002.

Lessons in Leadership

Great leaders set and articulate vision. Strategies and tactics are established to accomplish this vision. The best leaders "connect the dots." They articulate the "what, why, how, when, who" and explain how it fits into the overall mission. Many leaders fall into what I call a "series of random acts" instead of the comprehensive vision-strategy-tactics roadmap. As a result, they have inconsistent followership and poor execution. It's imperative to have a process to make decisions and execute strategies. Carter's error was that process was more important than outcomes. As a result, there was no appearance of clear vision or defining themes of his presidency.

Carter's commitment to education was admirable. He saw education as a significant key to bridging economic and social disparities. Leaders who are committed to learning continue to learn themselves.

It is only fitting to finish by acknowledging Carter's compassion for the disadvantaged. He clearly cared more for the flock than the fleece. His brand is that of a servant, a noble accomplishment for any leader.

CHAPTER 55

THE GIPPER

Ronald Reagan, 1981-1989

RONALD REAGAN, OUR 40TH president, was a highly influential voice of American conservatism. His path to the White House included being a radio broadcaster, actor, president of the Screen Actors Guild, and governor of California. He was elected president of the United States in 1980.

Reagan was known as "the great communicator." As a former sports announcer and actor, he used his excellent oratory skill to preach an ideology of optimism that influenced the nation and the world. His domestic economic policies were known as "Reaganomics." They favored reducing taxes and supporting free market activity. The philosophy of cutting taxes for the wealthy and having the benefits "trickle-down" to the rest of society became the platform for the future Republican party.

On the international front, Reagan used diplomacy to peacefully work with the collapsing government of the Soviet Union to create independence for the satellite countries of the former USSR. Of the fifteen satellite countries, fourteen chose democracies. Together with Soviet Premier Mikhail Gorbachev, Reagan also signed the Intermediate-Range Nuclear Forces (INF) Treaty, by which the two nations agreed to eliminate a large category of nuclear weapons.

Reagan was also known for making strong and somewhat controversial moves. He took unprecedented action on the Professional Air Traffic Controllers Organization strike in 1981 by firing the controllers and making them ineligible for federal services. He also abolished the FCC (Federal Communications Commission) Fairness Doctrine. The Fairness Doctrine, introduced in 1949, required that holders of broadcast licenses be held to a standard that all controversial issues of public importance were to be honest, equitable, and balanced. Repealing the law eliminated this standard and allowed cable and broadcast news to publish and promote as desired.[10]

A failure of Reagan's administration was his slow response to the AIDS crisis. Another questionable decision was his aid to the South African government despite their systematic discrimination against the majority black population, a practice known as Apartheid. Reagan later vetoed a bill to place sanctions on South Africa. Congress overrode the veto and enacted the Comprehensive Anti-Apartheid Act in 1986. Finally, his biggest failure was the Iran Contra Affair, the sale of arms to Iran during an embargo. The intent was to funnel proceeds of the sale to fund the Contras in Nicaragua after such funding had been prohibited by Congress.

Despite his failings, Ronald Reagan left office after two terms with one of the highest job approval ratings of any president.

Lessons in Leadership

Great leaders are great communicators. Ronald Reagan was an outstanding communicator who had an incredible ability to connect with people. Like all great leaders, he had a core message that was clear, concise, and consistent. Reagan took his tasks seriously, but not always himself seriously. He used humor and humility very effectively.

Ironically, another aspect of communication was, in hindsight, a Reagan failure. His dismantling of the FCC Fairness Doctrine has undoubtedly led to the polarization and reinforced public tribalism we deal with

---

10 In re Complaint of Syracuse Peach Council against Television Station WTVH Syracuse, New York, 2 FCC Rcd 5043 (1987).

today. One can't help but wonder if the founding fathers' concern over partisanship's risk to democracy was considered.

Great leaders are also motivators. Reagan brought optimism to the country that hadn't been there in a long time. Optimism became his brand, something that helped him in times of controversy. A strong brand is essential for the growth periods of an organization and even more important for when a leader stumbles—as we all do. As a result of his brand of optimism, Reagan had incredible followership.

Reagan also built partnerships "across the aisle" and was able to get things done as a result. He established strong relationships with international leaders, including Margaret Thatcher of Great Britain and Mikhail Gorbachev of the Soviet Union. He lived by a very disciplined approach to balance in life. He prioritized rest and relaxation. His opponents criticized him for that publicly and probably envied him for it privately. They, like all of us, need balance. You can't be or give your best if you are running on "fumes."

Reagan, for all his great qualities, had a few blind spots. One was from whom he took advice. While he had a capable cabinet and staff, he was heavily influenced by his wife Nancy and her "interesting" advisers. And while he was a visionary, he delegated the details. Great leaders know the details of core information, especially around things that matter.

CHAPTER 56

POPPY

George H.W. Bush, 1989-1993

GEORGE H.W. BUSH WAS very prepared to be our 41st president. He showed strong character and leadership ability early in his life. He joined the United States Navy on his 18th birthday and became a naval aviator. During World War II he served in the Pacific theater and was awarded the Distinguished Flying Cross for his heroism. After the war, he attended Yale University, where he was class president and captain of the baseball team. He graduated from Yale with a degree in economics and headed to West Texas to begin a career as an oil industry executive.

Bush won the Republican nomination for U.S. senator from Texas in 1964 but lost in the general election. He won a seat in the U.S. House of Representatives two years later. His resume also included being the U.S. ambassador to the United Nations, U.S. liaison to China, head of the CIA, and vice president of the United States under Ronald Reagan. He was elected to the presidency in 1988.

Bush's term in office was marked as a turning point on the world stage. The Berlin Wall came down, and Germany began the long process of reunification. The Soviet Union began to collapse, and the traditional Cold War ended. In response, Bush worked with Gorbachev, Premier of the Soviet Union, to sign a strategic arms reduction treaty.

Bush presided over two U.S. invasions: first in Panama, to overthrow a government that was seen as a potential threat to U.S. citizens there and to curb the drug trade into the U.S, and next in Iraq after the country invaded Kuwait, a neighboring ally of the U.S. At the time, both invasions were generally approved by the American public. These actions were positioned as a threat to our safety and, more importantly, a stand against troublesome dictators.

On the domestic front, Bush, a moderate conservative, did sign important legislation including the American Disabilities Act and the Clean Air Amendment. Unfortunately, he was not the inspiring leader his predecessor Ronald Reagan was. An economic recession harmed his approval. And, despite other accomplishments, if the country's economy isn't doing well and the public perceives the president's agenda as being responsible, that president won't get reelected. Bush is a prime example. Following his defeat in 1992, Bush was relegated to the club of one-term presidents.

With the reputation of being a consummate statesman and gentleman, Bush was awarded the Medal of Freedom by President Obama in 2011—a reflection of his service to our country.

Lessons in Leadership

Being a servant is one of the greatest attributes of a leader. It's not typically part of a job description or an important success factor. I've never known it to be any form of criteria for performance or pay. It is, however, an attribute every great leader should possess. George H.W. Bush was a decent person. He was a collaborator and gentleman. In many ways, he was the consummate servant to our county. That was his brand.

Leaders need to understand both risk and the root problem to be solved. Not thoroughly assessing potential outcomes can lead to settling only a near-term and not an underlying problem. Bush's two U.S. invasions are examples of this. My purpose is not to critique either invasion's legitimacy. Removing a bad dictator is probably a good thing. And drug trafficking certainly didn't change after the invasion of Panama. Both demand

and supply remain high to this day. As for Iraq, supporting your allies who have been invaded is part of longstanding U.S. policy.

Finally, great leaders inspire. They garner followership. Bush was a steady leader but unfortunately not inspiring. Following a highly inspirational leader, as Bush did with Reagan, shows us contrast. Those who have earned followership are most successful in shifting goals and directions. Bush was respected but not enthusiastically followed. We can see how this played out when he needed to change direction and raise taxes after having previously and famously promised: "read my lips—no new taxes." He didn't have the persona or followership to shift the change.

CHAPTER 57

BUBBA

William Jefferson Clinton, 1993-2001

WILLIAM JEFFERSON (BILL) CLINTON was the first baby-boomer generation president. He was also the first Democrat since FDR to be elected for two terms. Clinton came to office as a former lawyer, Arkansas attorney general, and governor of Arkansas. He rose to national attention as a long-shot candidate. As our nation's 42nd president, he led the country during a period of peace with an economy that underwent the largest expansion in history. He demonstrated a very flexible leadership style that was right of many of his Republican predecessors and left of his own party at times.

Clinton was an affable figure who was both loved and greatly distrusted. Some of the mistrust was self-inflicted. His first major effort in office was to overhaul healthcare. This had been a top Democratic agenda item since Truman was in office. The effort itself was not unusual. What was unusual was that he selected his wife Hillary to spearhead the effort and much of its design was absent Congressional Democrats' input. President Clinton was also investigated for his involvement in Whitewater, a real estate investment in vacation properties, early on in his presidency. These two events and the splintered support of his own party in passing the North American Free Trade Agreement (NAFTA) resulted in upheaval for the Democrats. The midterm elections of 1994 put the Republican party back into the majority in both the Senate and House of Representatives.

Despite his misfires and errors in judgment, Bill Clinton served in an almost "Goldilocks" environment. It was a golden age of technology coming to life, growth in Capitalism, and monetary control. The economy added nearly fifty thousand jobs per month during his first few years in office. Clinton realized the lowest unemployment in twenty-five years, and he cut taxes for almost fifteen million low-income families during this time. He improved public safety, adding more police. He enacted the Family Medical Leave Act (FMLA), which covered more than forty-two million Americans, reformed Welfare, and improved both affordability and accessibility to education. He not only improved our economy but also created a surplus in our budget, something that hasn't since been accomplished.

Clinton led the country during a period of relative world peace. He led the Oslo Accords, creating temporary peace between Palestine and Israel. He advocated for NATO's intervention in the Bosnian War and brokered a peace agreement. But he unfortunately turned his back on the Rwandan genocide, something he later greatly regretted.

Historians' assessment of Clinton is mixed. Despite a strong economy, robust job growth, a period of peace, and wealth expansion on "Main Street," his reputation stubbornly remained "untrustworthy." Not that he didn't earn the reputation. Clinton was impeached for lying to a grand jury about an affair with a White House intern. The public was generally more indifferent to his moral failure than his lying. The resulting lack of public trust overshadowed Clinton's overall successful presidency.

Lessons in Leadership

Great leaders adapt to get cooperation and consensus, especially when their opponent has a different agenda. Those who can draw both sides into the discussion to solicit feedback and create consensus bring other influencers to the table. Clinton missed this opportunity early on with healthcare reform. To his credit, he learned from this failure and successfully worked with the opposing party during his second term.

Remember that leadership is a speaking role. Great leaders are clear, inspire and console, and "connect the dots" to how strategies align with their vision. They relate to their audience, and the best make you feel like they are talking directly to you. Great communicators have a point. Bill Clinton was an outstanding communicator. He was masterful at relating to and connecting with his audience, both on stage and in small groups.

I am an introvert and was previously convinced that only extroverts were effective communicators. Over time I observed that some of the best public speakers are quite shy. I learned that the great ones practice. They have a clear, concise message, know their audience, and connect with them. They speak from the heart and establish credibility. It's a skill that can be developed. It's essential if you want to be an effective leader.

For his incredible intellect, communication skill, and political savvy, Clinton's Achille's heel was trust. Once trust is lost, your brand is damaged—sometimes permanently. Realizing we all can fail, the sooner we "come clean," the sooner we regain trust. This includes not trying to cover up but admitting your mistakes and apologizing—especially to those you've harmed. When you humble yourself, you will often be forgiven and given another chance. We are much more likely to trust someone who admits wrong than someone who tries to cover it up.

We live today in a time where leaders typically won't admit wrong-doings to protect against legal action. That may save them some short-term financial losses, but it certainly damages their brand in the long-term. Those who hide behind lawyers (with all due respect), flimsy policies, and distort laws are ultimately remembered for their weakness, not their courage.

CHAPTER 58

JUNIOR

George W. Bush, 2001-2009

GEORGE W. BUSH, OUR 43rd president, was the second of two elected father-son duos, the previous being John and John Quincy Adams. Bush was a two-term president after a narrow Supreme Court ruling gave him a controversial first-term victory. Bush was a former businessman, owner of the Texas Rangers baseball team, and governor of Texas. Thanks in large part to his father, Bush entered the 2000 presidential race with incredible name recognition.

Bush, a self-described "compassionate conservative," was forced to pivot his domestic agenda almost immediately. Less than one year into office, the United States was attacked by Islamic terrorists on September 11, 2001. This event changed not just the country's direction but also Bush's legacy.

After the attack on our nation, several significant events occurred. First was the U.S. invasion of Afghanistan. This invasion was intended to capture or kill the architect behind the attacks, Osama bin Laden, who was believed to be hiding in a Taliban stronghold between Afghanistan and Pakistan. Later, acting on what turned out to be faulty intelligence information, the U.S. invaded Iraq. This action overthrew a ruthless but stabilizing dictator and greatly disrupted the entire Middle East. These actions in both Afghanistan and Iraq were intended to avenge the attacks, eliminate threats, root out terrorism, and build democratic nations. Initially, the

American public supported the effort. But Bush's theme of nation-building was seen as very aggressive compared to actions of other presidents who followed the tenets of the Truman Doctrine. The conflicts in Iraq and Afghanistan ultimately led to instability, loss of life, and only near-term successes in defeating terrorism.

During this challenging time, Bush further responded by establishing the Department of Homeland Security and passing the Patriot Act. This act took the unprecedented step of increasing surveillance and limiting personal freedoms. The tactics used to enforce the Patriot Act used questionable methods of obtaining information and alienated allies worldwide.

On the domestic front, Bush's "no child left behind" educational effort was the most significant reform on our nation's education system in history. He expanded entitlements through the Medicare drug benefit. This most extensive expansion of the program since its creation during the Lyndon Johnson administration demonstrated Bush's compassionate side of being conservative. Bush also attempted to reform Social Security by partial privatization. This effort failed, but the story is far from over. Like Truman's failed effort to create healthcare for all, the issue of a growing entitlement built on a seventy-five-year-old philosophy will need to be addressed to maintain solvency.

At the end of his second term, the financial markets collapsed due to exuberant real estate speculation, undisciplined underwriting of mortgage-backed securities, poor oversight and adherence to regulations, and the worldwide appetite for higher yield investments. Many historians, economists, and barstool "experts" have written about this crisis. Most concur that it really boiled down to widespread greed and a weak regulatory environment. Bush probably could have tightened regulations when the massive bubble of the real estate market was forming, but I don't believe the blame for the crisis should fall solely on the Bush administration.

Bush inherited one of the largest surpluses in American history and left the office with one of the largest deficits. As measured by job creation, personal income, and even stock market performance, his record was one of the worst since the failed Hoover administration.

George W. Bush's largely overlooked yet most clearly compassionate decision was his massive debt forgiveness to many countries in Sub-Saharan Africa. This unprecedented gesture saved or greatly improved lives in one of the world's most vulnerable regions.

Lessons in Leadership

Great leaders need to step away from the emotion of the moment. They need to pause and seek wisdom before committing to something that dramatically impacts so many. In the aftermath of 9/11, George W. Bush showed that a calm, strong, determined, and clear message can reassure and galvanize a nation. On the other hand, while leaders need to focus on the important things that make a difference, being consumed by one issue at the expense of others can be harmful. In Bush's case, that was national security and revenge, which prevented him from focusing on his overall agenda.

Great leaders see all people as important and stand up for the greater good. In many cases, this means defending the most vulnerable. Bush's actions to expand Medicare prescription drugs and forgive African nations' debts were decisions that were generally not popular with his supporters or party. This is an example of being courageous and "doing the right thing."

Finally, who a leader surrounds themselves with shapes them. Bush was heavily influenced by a hawkish cabinet and had difficulty looking beyond their advice. Unfortunately, his vision for our country got altered along the way.

CONCLUSION

I have had the privilege of being in various leadership roles throughout my life. Most of my decisions, mistakes, successes, and failures have been relatively obscure. Even when leading thousands on a national level, I rarely faced public scrutiny. The forty-two men reviewed in this book held the highest office in the nation and one of the most powerful jobs in the world. They were constantly judged publicly. While the promise of life, liberty and the pursuit of happiness may be our nation's founding vision, the needs, opinions, and issues vary greatly among the millions of people who comprise this great country. Political parties hold much sway in influencing the voting public. The media places any policy, position, statement, or decision in the immediate hands of the public. Overlay that with massive pressure from lobbyists and donors and holding title in the Executive Office of the president of the United States becomes a far more complex role than a leadership handbook could ever cover.

I believe these forty-two men all loved our country. All of them did what they felt was best for the nation. Some who led during the early periods of the formation of our government were literally taking an experiment, untried and unproven, and building a republic without a blueprint.

As different as each of these men were, they had some common traits. All of them wanted the republic to flourish. They wanted America to remain free. They all viewed the Constitution, albeit through different lenses, as being a guiding template. And while some pushed the limits of their powers more than others, they respected the balance of power our government was built on.

In writing this book, my intention was to note a few accomplishments and failures of each president and reflect on the leadership lessons from each. As a reflective citizen and not a historian, I realize I may not have included or expanded on issues some may see as worthy. After reading this book, a critic might suggest that I should have taken a deeper dive into each's background, for instance. I have no doubt that a person's background plays an extremely important role in what shapes them, but my interest has always been in relaying what effective leadership looks like, regardless of presidential origin stories.

The lessons in leadership presented in this book use a combination of my own principles applied to the actions of the presidents. One challenge in doing this was the knowledge that to truly judge an action one needs to look at the long-term impact on society and how presidential decisions influenced it. There will be disagreement here, too.

It became apparent to me that several of the less-acclaimed presidents could have been outstanding given different circumstances. Others showed their true character and lack of leadership skill when given power that they then misused. Both scenarios are common in corporate America as well as in the business world in general. In fact, you might be struggling with them in your life right now.

Not everyone should lead people, least of all become president of the United States. Leadership is a privilege that comes with incredible responsibility. Leaders directly and indirectly impact the lives of others. What they do and how they do it can have lasting consequences. Whether a person is formally leading others or is an individual influencer, it is important not to lose sight of the responsibility that comes with the role.

Great leaders consciously identify principles and behaviors that guide them. The best ones develop and improve the skills necessary to execute those principles and instill them in those they lead. There are many excellent principles that successful leaders live by and lead with. Mine are certainly not reflective of all the lessons I have learned and adopted along my journey; they are the foundation. I share them once again here:

1. Care for the flock, not the fleece

2. Create and communicate a vision and plan

3. Focus on a few well-done items to make a big difference

4. Always know your audience

5. Avoid hubris

6. Maintain balance and don't waste a good worry

7. Be curious and continue to learn

8. Build followership

9. Be courageous

10. Brand matters.

I hope you walk away from this book knowing a little more about those who served in the White House. Since this is first and foremost a book on leadership, I hope that the leadership lessons, when applied to my reflections on the presidents, become more apparent and useful in your life and career. Most of us will never be president or even a leader with a significant following. But never forget: we are all leaders in some way.

I encourage every leader to establish their own fundamental principles that guide them. Great leaders impact lives in countless ways. To those who honor the role and the people they serve, cast a vision, do important things well, communicate clearly and effectively, stay humble, stay steady in the storms of life, keep learning, surround themselves with the best, and develop them, and remain courageous, I salute you.

ACKNOWLEDGMENTS

To those who inspired and encouraged me in my formative years, Amy, Willy, and Gunnar. Thank you for "seeing" me.

To the business leaders who took a chance on me and always had my back as I learned, Bill, Pat, and Jay. Thank you for believing in me.

To all the "big middle" influencers of life. Thank you for your everyday acts of kindness and wisdom that make us all better.

To those who provided valuable feedback for this book, Carmie, Denise, Greg, Karen, and Morrison. Thank you for your insights, honesty, and skill.

To my outstanding editor, Greg. Thank you for your expertise and for helping to make my dream a reality.

To my mother, Ramona. Thank you for showing me what a servant leader looks like.

To my wife, Terri. Thank you for always encouraging me and artfully helping shape my words.

To Isaac, Tia, and Benji. You are my inspiration for a bright future.

And finally, Soli Deo Gloria, "He alone is worthy."

FOR FURTHER DISCUSSION

1. What motivates you as a leader? How do you test your perception against reality?

2. What circumstances have you faced as a leader that have required you to stand on a principle? How did you handle it?

3. Why are some partnerships so challenging to maintain? What are you doing to develop the most difficult ones?

4. How do you tackle issues you don't fully understand?

5. Which areas of learning would be beneficial for you to explore further, both personally and professionally? Which areas are stagnant?

6. How do you know when a person or group is following your lead? How do you identify and overcome reluctant followership?

7. What are some things you do to restore yourself? What does balance look like to you?

8. Whom have you observed that is truly a courageous leader?

9. How does being courageous differ from being egotistical or obstinate?

10. What do you think is your brand? What would your co-workers say? What would your family and friends say?

11. How do you prioritize what is most important? How do you identify root issues?

12. Do you have your current team members in the right positions and places?

13. If you were to start your own company today, would you take your current team with you? Why or why not?

14. Think of a time you made a mistake. What did you learn from the error? Did you admit it to your team? Why or why not?

15. How would you rate your communication skill? What are you doing to develop that skill?

REFERENCES

Ambrose, Stephen E. "Eisenhower: Soldier and President (The renowned one-volume life)." Simon Schuster, New York (1990).

Baker, Jean H. James Buchanan: The American Presidents Series: The 15th President, 1857-1861. Macmillan, 2004.

Brands, Henry William. Woodrow Wilson: The American Presidents Series: The 28th President, 1913-1921. Vol. 28. Macmillan, 2003.

Brinkley, Douglas. Gerald R. Ford: The American Presidents Series: The 38th President, 1974-1977. Macmillan, 2007.

Calhoun, Charles W., and Charles William Calhoun. Benjamin Harrison: The American Presidents Series: The 23rd President, 1889-1893. Vol. 23. Macmillan, 2005.

Cheney, Lynne. James Madison: A life reconsidered. Penguin, 2014.

Chernow, Ron. Grant. Head of Zeus Ltd, 2017.

Chernow, Ron. Washington: A Life. Penguin, 2010.

Collins, Gail. William Henry Harrison: The American Presidents Series: The 9th President, 1841. Macmillan, 2012.

Dallek, Robert. Franklin D. Roosevelt: A Political Life. Penguin, 2017.

Dallek, Robert. An Unfinished Life: John F. Kennedy, 1917-1963. Hachette UK, 2003.

Dalton, C. David. "Ronald C. White, Jr.: A. Lincoln: A Biography." Teaching History: A Journal of Methods 35, no. 1 (2010): 51-53.

Dean, John W. Warren G. Harding: The American Presidents Series: The 29th President, 1921-1923. Macmillan, 2004.

Eisenhower, John SD. Zachary Taylor: The American Presidents Series: The 12th President, 1849-1850. Macmillan, 2008.

Farrell, John A. Richard Nixon: The Life. Vintage, 2017.

Finkelman, Paul. Millard Fillmore: The American Presidents Series: The 13th President, 1850-1853. Macmillan, 2011.

Goodwin, Doris Kearns. "Lyndon Johnson and the American Dream. New York: St." Martin's Griffin (1991).

Goodwin, Doris Kearns. Team of rivals: The political genius of Abraham Lincoln. Penguin UK, 2009.

Gordon-Reed, Annette. Andrew Johnson: The American Presidents Series: The 17th President, 1865-1869. Vol. 17. Macmillan, 2011.

Graff, Henry F., and Henry Franklin Graff. Grover Cleveland: The American Presidents Series: The 22nd and 24th President, 1885-1889 and 1893-1897. Macmillan, 2002.

Greenberg, David. Calvin Coolidge: The American Presidents Series: The 30th President, 1923-1929. Macmillan, 2006.

Hart, Gary. 5. James Monroe. New York University Press, 2016.

Holt, Michael F. Franklin Pierce: The American Presidents Series: The 14th President, 1853-1857. Macmillan, 2010.

Kaplan, Fred. John Quincy Adams: American Visionary. Harper Collins, 2014.

Karabell, Zachary. Chester Alan Arthur: The American Presidents Series: The 21st President, 1881-1885. Macmillan, 2004.

Leuchtenburg, William E. Herbert Hoover: The American Presidents Series: The 31st President, 1929-1933. Macmillan, 2009.

Mann, James. George W. Bush: The American Presidents Series: The 43rd President, 2001-2009. Times Books, 2015.

May, Gary. John Tyler: The American Presidents Series: The 10th President, 1841-1845. Vol. 10. Macmillan, 2008.

McPherson, James M., and George Henry Davis. Tried by war: Abraham Lincoln as commander in chief. Penguin, 2008Meacham, Jon. Thomas Jefferson: The art of power. Random House Incorporated, 2012.

McCullough, David. John Adams. Simon and Schuster, 2002.

McCullough, David. Truman. Simon and Schuster, 2003

Phillips, Kevin. William McKinley: The American Presidents Series: The 25th President, 1897-1901. Times Books, 2014.

Pringle, Henry F. Theodore Roosevelt. 1931.

Roberts, Andrew. Leadership in War: Lessons from Those Who Made History. Penguin UK, 2019.

Rosen, Jeffrey. William Howard Taft: The American Presidents Series: The 27th President, 1909-1913. Times Books, 2018.

Rove, Karl. The Triumph of William McKinley: Why the Election of 1896 Still Matters. Simon and Schuster, 2015.

Rutkow, Ira. James A. Garfield: The American Presidents Series: The 20th President, 1881. Macmillan, 2006.

Seigenthaler, John. James K. Polk: The American Presidents Series: The 11th President, 1845-1849. Vol. 11. Macmillan, 2004.

Spitz, Bob. Reagan: An American Journey. Penguin Books, 2019.

Tomasky, Michael. Bill Clinton: The American Presidents Series: The 42nd President, 1993-2001. Macmillan, 2017.

Ward, Geoffrey C. The Roosevelts: An Intimate History. Knopf, 2014.

Widmer, Ted. Martin Van Buren: The American Presidents Series: The 8th President, 1837-1841. Macmillan, 2005.

Zelizer, Julian E. Jimmy Carter: The American Presidents Series: The 39th President, 1977-1981. Macmillan, 2010.

ABOUT THE AUTHOR

Tim Traudt grew up in Central Nebraska and spent his adult life in the Twin Cities of Minneapolis and St. Paul, Minnesota. From his first paper route at nine years old to retiring as a financial services executive more than fifty years later, Tim has always been drawn to the concept of leadership and what causes people to follow others.

Tim is an avid reader, sports fan, worldwide traveler, Peloton® rider, follower of Jesus, and history junkie. He has served on numerous boards and been actively involved in several charitable efforts across the globe. Tim and his wife Terri live in Edina, Minnesota.

Executive Office combines his passion for leadership and American history. It is Tim's first book.